P9-BVG-767

Emily Brontë

EMILY BRONTË
A Critical and Biographical Study

♣

John Hewish

Macmillan
St Martin's Press

© John Hewish 1969

First edition 1969
Reprinted 1971

Published by
THE MACMILLAN PRESS LTD
London and Basingstoke
Associated companies in New York Toronto
Dublin Melbourne Johannesburg and Madras

Library of Congress catalog card no. 76–85143

SBN 333 04417 7

Printed in Great Britain by
REDWOOD PRESS LIMITED
Trowbridge & London

For a poet with dramatic gifts, a situation quite remote from his personal experience may release the strongest emotion.

T. S. ELIOT 'In Memoriam'

Contents

Preface

The potential interest of my subject is, I hope, self-evident. Emily Brontë has long been referred to in very good literary company, and *Wuthering Heights* is a great classic as well as one of the most popular novels in the language. But it is also among the more inaccessible and controversial of books. The last word on a novel that combines these qualities has certainly not been said.

Emily Brontë also has the reputation of being a somewhat perilous subject. Many critics, in the last century and in this, have tended to fight shy of lengthy treatment of any of the Brontës, or have contented themselves with a passing reference or brief 'placing'. The reasons for their restraint are clearer to me now than at the outset. Emily Brontë died young. Such unfulfilled prodigies present special difficulties of judgement. But difficulties arise also from the kind of person and writer she was. Her work is introspective and is characterised by a clash between a rigid and orthodox moral background and a tendency to emotional extremes. The cryptic, private expression of her moral originality in the poems resembles Blake's. In her case, too, one must trust the tale, since the author left so little of herself (much less than Blake did) to trust her by. As for the tale, apart from the poet's novel, *Wuthering Heights*, it was never intended for publication. This author's life and personality are monolithic and tend to be biographer-proof.

There have been some incentives, apart from the personal factors that enter into a subject's choice of an author. To cite the Brontë industry here may seem unguarded, but understanding of the Brontës, and, of course, of Victorian literature, has made progress since the last study of Emily in book form and in English. Many of the most interesting contributions are either in specialist periodicals or are out of print. The poems, available since 1941 in chronological arrangement in Hatfield's edition, are an extensive, intimate and unique source, which has only recently received much attention. There has also been a tendency to declare Emily Brontë's life a mystery and to leave it at that. It has, I think, been suspected for some time that her sister's brief account of it, and of her character, is not altogether satisfactory, but it prevails in most of the editions of her works.

The claims implicit in these remarks should not be over-estimated. My biographical outline should be taken as such, and not as an attempted full or 'definitive' life. Some well-loved passages in the records are (for that very reason) curtailed or excluded. My use of the poems may have led to some repetitiveness, but there is no comparable evidence, and it seemed that there may be some value in using them chronologically. I have not been in the lucky position of having an unworked mine of material. As I have predominantly depended on published versions of the poems, letters and prose notes, the dates and transcripts should not be taken as absolutely authoritative without further reference to manuscript sources. (Anyone with much experience of the Brontë records will understand this proviso.) However, wherever readily available the original manuscripts or facsimiles were used.

Many of the biographical problems, such as the dating of *Wuthering Heights* and the related facts of the transition (or alternation) from Gondal poet to novelist, cannot at present be solved – at least I have not solved them. My account of the origins of Gondal is much indebted to the work of Miss Ratchford, though I deplore the kind of approach suggested by the title *Gondal's Queen – A Novel in Verse*. If I have taken advantage of her studies and those of other Brontë scholars without adequate acknowledgement I apologise in advance for such transgressions. Anyone attempting a general study of any of the Brontës must inevitably owe a great debt to the discoveries and insights of more than a century of biography and criticism. He is very fortunate and percipient if he can add to them.

J. H.

Acknowledgements

I am indebted to the following for access to and/or permission to transcribe and quote from manuscripts and other material: the Council of the Brontë Society; the Keeper of Manuscripts, British Museum; the late Dr J. D. Gordan, Curator of the Berg Collection, New York Public Library.

Thanks are also especially due to the following: Mrs Hutton, Curator of the Brontë Parsonage Museum, Haworth, for much help and encouragement; Ian Willison, Assistant Keeper, Department of Printed Books, British Museum, for invaluable help; P. N. Furbank and Miss Elizabeth Ellem for editorial assistance and encouragement; Professor W. Houghton and others (especially Henry Rosenberg) concerned with the Wellesley Index; the late Sir John Murray for access to Brontë correspondence; Miss Amy G. Foster, Secretary of the Yorkshire Archaeological Society, Leeds; the Assistant Keeper, the Brotherton Library; W. J. Macdonald, Keeper of the Records, British Transport Historical Records, York; H. S. Linfield, for bibliographical help; Miss Hilda Marsden; John Willett; T. I. Rae, National Library of Scotland, for references from *Blackwood's* Contributors' Book; A. N. Harrison, archivist of Barclays Bank Ltd.

Special thanks are also due to many librarians, notably those of the British Museum Reading Room, North Library and Newspaper Library; the Public Record Office and National Register of Archives; the Guildhall Library; the Senate House Library and (not least) those of the London boroughs of Camden, Westminster and St Marylebone.

The extracts from Emily Brontë's essays 'Le Chat' and 'Le Papillon' are from the unpublished manuscripts in the Henry W.

and Albert A. Berg Collection of the New York Public Library, Astor, Lenox and Tilden Foundations.

I also wish to thank Columbia University Press, New York, for permission to quote from *The Complete Poems of Emily Jane Brontë*, edited by C. W. Hatfield, 1941. When quoting the poems the now conventional practice of giving each poem quoted its number in the Hatfield edition has been followed. In most cases the familiar title, if any, of the poem is given or – where untitled – the first line.

Introduction: The Sources

The Brontës' sudden fame and early deaths, combined with a certain native aloofness, aroused the curiosity of their contemporaries. One result was an unusually large proportion of secondary material, often originating from those less intimate with the family than they claimed to be. On the other hand there is an unusual lack of first-hand records, such as journals from the Brontës themselves: individual experience on even a single day of unworldly lives is extensive and varied. What a lot of their days there are of which we know nothing! They were, however, among the closest of the literary circles that seem almost characteristic of the age of romanticism. Literature is a predatory art, and the sources, including (with reservations) the novels, are both richer and riskier to interpret because the sisters and brother wrote about each other.

In one of her three known letters, all short, Emily Brontë wrote that the production of a proper letter was a feat she had 'never performed',[1] so there is no reason to think that these are the tip of an iceberg. She was at first reluctant for even her formal works to be published. She presents the unusual, but by no means unique, case of one for whom writing was an essential act of creation and recording that stopped short at communication itself. Her worked-over, carefully copied and secret poetry manuscripts remind one of Pascal's testament, sewn into his coat lining, though a certain contradictoriness can be detected in her attitude to disclosure of her poems and *Wuthering Heights*. It is not surprising that personal records, public or private, are almost non-existent, and her daily life and circumstances must be approached largely at second hand. This means principally through Charlotte Brontë's letters and the memoirs of the few who knew her, such as Ellen Nussey, Mary Taylor and M. Heger.

It was probably custom, rather than acumen, that caused Ellen Nussey to keep so many of Charlotte's letters. They met when Charlotte went to Miss Wooler's school in January 1831. This friendship with the pious, conventional Miss Nussey surprisingly lasted for the rest of Charlotte's life. In a declaration of loyalty she failed to explain it: 'she is no more than a conscientious, well-bred Yorkshire girl, she is without romance'.[2] The relationship perhaps provided the element of normality that the Brontë temperament found solace in, and which a relationship with, say, the critic Sydney Dobell (which was offered) would have lacked. Ellen Nussey was not fully intimate with Charlotte Brontë, even less with Currer Bell, but the letters are the main source on the family before the transformation from one to the other, after which Charlotte's circle widened. With the emergence of Currer Bell these new relationships provide more information about her sisters, as she is in the great tradition of indefatigable Victorian correspondents.

Ellen Nussey's character is a complete contrast to that of the Brontës. She was sucked into the flame, to suffer for it for the rest of her life. Her own published account goes back to their time at Roe Head school, 1831–3; it appeared first in *Scribner's Monthly*, in America, in 1871, or forty years later, after the Brontë novels and after Mrs Gaskell's *Life of Charlotte Brontë* (in the research for which, of course, she had co-operated).

Though she knew the family as well as anyone, Ellen Nussey, like the rest of their circle, was not very close to Emily. There is, too, a certain derivative flavour about her reminiscences, in addition to that of naïve authenticity. Her description of the parsonage is a setting for domestic romance: 'mind and thought, I had almost said elegance, but certainly refinement, diffused themselves over all'.[3] As the 'mine whence writers on the Brontës have drawn their ore'[4] she felt understandably exploited, and attempted her own edition of the letters. It had to be destroyed, because Clement Shorter bought the copyright in the letters from Charlotte's widower, Arthur Nicholls, who was very deferent to such literary personalities.

No account of the sources can omit Mrs Gaskell's *Life*, or her recently published *Letters*, edited by J. A. V. Chapple and Arthur Pollard. As official biographer she enjoyed a uniquely favourable position. It is still unwise to claim biographical discoveries before taking another look at Mrs Gaskell. The enduring value of the *Life* is largely in her sophistication and social sense, her feel for the dramatic and for the regional background. But this inevitably no longer sacrosanct work was, perhaps, published too soon; it was certainly written too quickly. In spite of her painstaking research, it contains many inadvertent inaccuracies, as well as its well-known suppressions and pieties. (It is important to distinguish between the first and the toned-down editions.) Mrs Gaskell was not, of course, a critic. What would G. H. Lewes have made of the material – amd of Emily Brontë – had he undertaken more than occasional reviewing of the Brontës' works?

The Life of Charlotte Brontë was commenced some months after its subject's death in 1855. Mrs Gaskell met Charlotte in the early 1850s, and her first impressions of her, of Haworth, Mr Brontë and the parsonage are especially interesting as the first from such an observer; their obvious excitement conveys the degree of curiosity about the family. A taste for the romantic, admiration of self-help and the feminine ideal were all satisfied. One can't, however, dispel an impression that the warm-hearted Mrs Gaskell, who admired Charlotte's moral strength so much, tended to take first impressions for the whole truth, and was too receptive to casual opinion.

By the time Mrs Gaskell met Charlotte, Emily was dead. But, from what she was told, Emily's character made a tremendous impression on her: 'I told her of —'s admiration for *Shirley*, which pleased her, for the character of Shirley was meant for her sister Emily, about whom she is never tired of talking, nor I of listening. Emily must have been a remnant of the Titans . . .'[5]

Emily the writer impressed her hardly at all, but as second to her main subject Emily the person is treated without sentiment. Her brief appearances in the *Life* are all the more valuable for that.

There is, of course, an Emily Brontë myth, consisting of anecdotes related in various books. Many of these happenings are in character; the problems begin when one tries to find them in the primary sources. That they were not reported by members of the family does not make them untrue; it does make them less authoritative.

Local anecdote was retailed as fact by several biographers, from Mary Robinson onwards. Some stories suggest mythopoeia from the Brontës' published works. For instance, Ellen Nussey (in her memoir of 1871) states that Emily combined study with the baking, with books 'a common sight in the kitchen'.[6] Earlier Mrs Gaskell (published 1857) wrote that Emily studied German 'out of an open book propped before her'.[7] Was 'anyone passing by the kitchen door' in this version Ellen Nussey, from whom Mrs Gaskell may have obtained the story, or did Ellen get it from Mrs Gaskell, who was published first, or did (as one can't help wondering) the anecdote originate in *Jane Eyre*,[8] in which the Rivers sisters are seen reading German – but not baking – and where Diana, who resembles Emily, declaims from Schiller's *Die Räuber*? 'Emily does most of the baking', Charlotte recorded in a letter,[9] but further the primary evidence does not go. The Brontës provide an example of one aspect of the historical process. But it does not do in such cases to be too hot for certainties. Many of the stories, like the one just examined, are appropriate and may well be true.

Before criticising Charlotte as a witness in her sister's case it is salutary to remember that Emily as writer was her discovery, and that without her the Brontës might never have been heard of. By now I suppose that the merits and deficiencies of Charlotte's account of her sisters – affectionate, somewhat patronising and not always accurate or showing complete understanding – are fairly well recognised. In her dominant position as survivor and editor she combined, in the biographical prefaces and elsewhere, some of the insights that she alone could provide, with a very Victorian doing of the obsequies: she tended to keep the younger ones in their place. (Over-zealous literary executorship is not uncommon, particularly perhaps in the nineteenth century.) Emily's genius and reserve fascinated and baffled Charlotte. After her sisters' deaths her position was strange and tragic. She was left to edit and present their works, with a deepening sense of Emily's importance as writer, even in the widely misunderstood and underrated *Wuthering Heights*, and with the knowledge that the grave had set the seal on that lifetime of reserve. *Shirley* had been commenced before Emily died. It seems possible that it became an exorcising of this ghost, in the sense that in putting a person in a novel you possess or are defended against them. Charlotte displayed all her characteristic fortitude in these circumstances, but the time was unfavourable to the task. Her letters indicate that this commission from her publisher came to have a therapeutic function: 'I am busy now – Mr Smith wishes to reprint some of Emily's and Anne's works . . . I have been closely engaged in revising . . . I found the task exquisitely painful and depressing – now regarding it in the light of a *sacred* duty.'[10]

The unfortunate emendations to *Wuthering Heights* (and to an even greater extent to the poems) that resulted were well meant. Luckily they were not irremediable, but her normally excellent ear deserted her. 'That labor limae that Currer lacks, Ellis has',[11] she had modestly written, when defending Emily against an insensitive review. The question of the lost papers of Emily and Anne remains open: they may have been destroyed by their authors, by Charlotte or her husband or by none of these. In Charlotte's prefaces, facts of interest concerning Emily's life are omitted, or the emphasis, as indicated by other evidence, is altered. The Notice published with the 1850 edition of *Wuthering Heights* contains a just appreciation of the poetry, Charlotte's discovery, but she gives and takes away in characteristically Victorian fashion. An ostensible defence of the reputation of Ellis and Acton Bell becomes a disclaimer of responsibility for the 'inferior' and 'immature' *Wuthering Heights*, and the 'entire mistake'[12] of *The Tenant of Wildfell Hall*. The story told by Mrs Gaskell (in a letter) of Emily broken-hearted by the reviews of *Wuthering Heights* does not fit the facts either. 'But Emily – poor Emily – the pangs of disappointment as review after review came out about *Wuthering Heights* were terrible. Miss B. said she had no recollection of pleasure or gladness about *Jane Eyre*, every such feeling was lost . . .'[13] Emily did not live to see the more perceptive reviews of *Wuthering Heights*, but this account gives a false impression, even of the earliest ones, some of which she certainly saw. Emily and Anne Brontë were not snuffed out by an article.

The history of the Brontë papers resembles a story by Henry James. 'We carried away with us a whole heap of those minute writings', Mrs Gaskell informed Emily Shaen in 1856,[14] but it was left to Thomas J. Wise and Clement Shorter to obtain the bulk of the still unpublished manuscripts from Charlotte's widower some forty years later, in 1895. Shorter visited Mr Nicholls (then in retirement at Banagher in Ireland) many times. He reported after the first visit that the latter had placed all the papers in his possession into his hands. They were more varied and abundant than he could possibly have anticipated, he wrote.[15] They included much early writing by Charlotte and Branwell, Emily's manuscript book of 'personal' poems, and other poetry manuscripts. Further application to Nicholls produced the 1841 and 1845 'birthday notes'. The division of much of this material into small lots and its dispersal by sale has aggravated the editorial problem. In her 'Census of Brontë MSS in the United States of America', Miss M. G. Christian reports that the manuscripts are dispersed from New England to Hawaii, and from the Middle West to Texas. The characteristic small script in which most of the manuscripts are written is difficult to transcribe and identify, and there are several wrong ascriptions in the material bound for Wise or edited for publication by Shorter. (Miss Christian reviews the history of the manuscripts in the work mentioned.) These factors, and its own peculiar character, helped to conceal the real nature of Emily's poetry – and of the childhood writing as a whole – until well into this century.

The present standard, if not definitive, edition for the biographer is the Shakespeare Head Brontë, which includes four volumes of letters and other material. The work of Wise, Symington, Shorter and Hatfield during the 1930s, the SHB is the 'best edition we have', of impressive scope, but it is not a work of scholarship by current standards, The transcriptions have been faulted, and some of the commentary is lifted direct from much earlier works, such as Shorter's, and Mary Robinson's *Emily Brontë*. The dating of certain letters (important as regards the life of Emily Brontë) is problematic: many of Charlotte's were sent without full dates, and were given conjectural dates by Ellen Nussey, Mrs Gaskell and others. Dates in Shorter's (1908) edition and in the SHB sometimes differ (unaccountably, since Shorter had had a hand in the latter). The SHB is a remarkable and perhaps never to be repeated lucky-dip. (I believe that a new edition of the letters is being prepared by Miss Christian; meanwhile she does not answer mine.)

Evidently, the resources of the average student or researcher would be insufficient to locate the originals of all the material for which originals exist, but even limited research has its uses in this field. From the English translations of Emily Brontë's essays in French one would not suspect that she wrote anything but impeccably in that language: in fact, as a pupil, she wrote the French a pupil writes. 'Best plays are secret plays', Charlotte is supposed to have written, according to Mrs Gaskell[16] and others. Not so, but 'bed plays'. There is no adequate edition of the Brontë juvenilia, though the two volumes in the SHB are useful. Hatfield's *The Complete Poems of Emily Jane Brontë* set an editorial example few have followed. The doubtful poems are primarily those printed from Shorter's transcripts, and are of minor importance. Emily Brontë's practice of dating her poems, usually to the day, is helpful, but also somewhat tantalising. Are we to suppose that the 150 lines commencing 'Silent is the House' were written in a day? The Hatfield edition has recently been reprinted by the Oxford University Press without revision, though some minor defects have been pointed out in print (notably by Miss Christian and W. D. Paden) and without taking advantage of recent studies of Gondal. It is a pity that an edition with the status of the Penguin English Library *Wuthering Heights* has various minor inaccuracies, a disputed portrait on the cover and a text marred by many literals.

Many important Brontë manuscripts are still in England, at the British Museum, at Haworth and elsewhere. Among those not in public collections is the 'Honresfeld' manuscript of Emily's poems. This or its companion transcript-book was the volume found by Charlotte and which inspired their first approaches to publishers. I understand that it is still owned by a descendant of Sir Alfred Law, who obtained it from Wise, but that its location is secret. Fortunately it was carefully transcribed by Davidson Cook, who published an account of it in 1926. The editors of the Shakespeare Head edition also included useful facsimiles of all these poems, making it possible to study Emily's second thoughts, and Charlotte's alterations. Shorter's *The Complete Works of Emily Jane Brontë* (1910–11) also contains important facsimiles. There have been few recent finds relating to Emily: the most important are, perhaps, two early diary-notes (both published in *Brontë Society Transactions*). The importance of her French essays is out of all proportion to their extent, because of the lack of other such records. The manuscript of *Wuthering Heights* is lost.

It is now just one hundred and fifty years since the birth of Emily Brontë. Anyone closely involved with the Brontë literature produced during this period may well echo Charlotte's 'I feel as if we were all buried here.'[17] There have been many additions to it while this study was in preparation. For a more complete survey the reader can refer to Miss Christian's chapter in *Victorian Fiction, a guide to research*, edited by L. Stevenson (1964).

BOOK ONE
The Life

I

IN SOME ways, certainly, Emily Brontë's life and work seem unusually of a piece, in exemplifying extremes. Her withdrawal from close relationships outside the family – and to some extent within it – was combined with an essentially religious or philosophic preoccupation with the meaning of human existence. She was a recluse who spent much of the time remaining from household chores in writing, but not for publication. She allowed her work to be published only as a concession to her sisters' project. Her life, though her character lent it a certain drama, was mysterious, mainly because genius in an unobtrusive life is apt in time to seem so.

The background of the family and the outline of their story is familiar. Patrick Brontë's forebears were uncultivated, and he was unremarkable intellectually, but his character commands attention. He owed his 'further education' and position to his own efforts and to the Evangelical movement. His change of name was a romantic gesture, and his drive as a young man combined self-help with the ability to obtain help from others. He was a 'Simeonite' (a poor ordinand of St John's College, Cambridge).[1] Their position was defined by Samuel Butler: 'To most of them, the fact of becoming clergymen would be the entrée into a social position from which they were at present kept out by barriers they well knew to be impassable.'[2]

The atmosphere of the sisters' upbringing and their social background were thus profoundly influenced by the last great religious movement in England, and by that earlier manifestation of Puritanism, Methodism (which influenced Mr Brontë's own early life: it was the religion of his relatives by marriage, and was strong in Yorkshire). This spiritual revival was related to romanticism.

The imagination and fervour that helped him to become an Evangelical clergyman reappear in the general character of his daughters' works.

The family moved to Haworth in early 1820, when Emily, born at Thornton, Bradford (30 July 1818), during Mr Brontë's previous curacy, was not two years old. *La race, le milieu, le moment* – their genius is not, of course, fully accounted for in these terms, though they now seem inseparable from the nineteenth-century isolation of Haworth, just as, in a minor sense, their works are inseparable from Yorkshire. But they did not accept Yorkshire, there was a stress between the sensitivity, the visionary element in their alien race and the human millstone-grit of this milieu. Emily Brontë as novelist could hardly have been less of a realist, but her materials in *Wuthering Heights* combine regional and literary elements. The melodramatic setting of the parsonage, between churchyard and the moorland paradigm of elemental nature, seems particularly appropriate just at this period: it embodies the intellectual and spiritual preoccupations of the early nineteenth century. Nor was this exclusively an arcadian isolation; Haworth was part of the industrial area of the West Riding. Mrs Brontë, whom Patrick married in 1812 as Maria Branwell, died in 1821. It was the first of the series of bereavements that darkened the family story, even in an age familiar with premature death. Her sister, Elizabeth, shortly after took charge and stayed until her death in 1842. In 1821 she was forty-six, and possessed a small private income,[3] so the parsonage, in a region she is said to have disliked, may have been a refuge as well as an outlet for good works. Certainly she showed no more inclination to leave it than her brother-in-law. The records that might have given Miss Branwell's stern portrait a voice are not available. She is a more obscure and slighter figure than the father. She was a Methodist, whose relatives married men active in sectarian education and missionary work, contributors to the superstitious magazines that roused the adult Brontës' scorn.[4]

Mr Brontë tried unsuccessfully to re-marry. (Goethe's dictum that 'opportunity occasions relationships' applies strikingly to several of the family.) Both he and Miss Branwell are still somewhat controversial characters. The children grew up motherless, closely confined with an already middle-aged father, himself something of a recluse, and an elderly and not very sympathetic aunt. They became intellectually precocious and socially immature.

Their attitudes to their home were mixed, and provide an interesting if special example of the position of women in the early Victorian period: they combined intense attachment and pride, with tension and revolt: 'pleasure and I had never met', relates Crimsworth, in Charlotte Brontë's *The Professor*, 'no indulgence of hers had enervated or sated one faculty of my nature. Liberty I clasped in my arms for the first time.'[5]

Charlotte Brontë chafed, escaped, and returned to chafe again, but nevertheless asked Mrs Gaskell whether the social round did not interfere with artistic integrity, the 'severe truth'.[6] Soon after coming to Haworth her father wrote: 'I have not tried to make any friends, nor have I met with any whose mind is congenial with my own.'[7] The disclosure might be by Emily, the most complete recluse of them all, who erected near-impregnable defences against such normality as Charlotte often yielded to. Her poetry reveals the occasional stress all the same, as does the sometimes gratuitous violence of *Wuthering Heights*, which recalls some of the anecdotes about its author. The frustration of so many Victorian women became a source of power in the Brontës' works, but the essential soil of their art also gives rise to certain limitations.

Emily joined her three sisters at the semi-charitable Clergy Daughters' School in November 1824, when she was just over six. The tragic deaths of the two elder daughters, first Maria then Elizabeth, resulted in Mr Brontë removing Charlotte and Emily in June of the following year. If Emily remembered Cowan Bridge she made no direct reference to it of the kind recorded by her sister, though one notes the doomed, outcast or unwanted children of the Gondal poems and *Wuthering Heights*. She was the youngest of the family to be exposed to the teaching and administration of the Rev. William Carus Wilson, who was a religious fanatic[8] (in an age of such fanatics). His writings

contain enough in the Brocklehurst vein to confirm Charlotte's
version of him, and his Calvinism perturbed other prominent
Evangelicals, such as the Rev. Charles Simeon, another patron of
the Clergy Daughters' School.[9] Anne, who did not attend the
school, suffered as much from religious morbidity as her sisters.
More serious, perhaps, than the effect of one clergyman, whom
Charlotte certainly never forgot, was the loss of the elder sisters,
Maria and Elizabeth.

Patrick Brontë, as noted, was no dilettante Evangelical like many
in a fashionable movement, but a first-graft enthusiast. His moral
role as father was reinforced by his being, as Butler put it of a
comparable situation, 'so much at home or close about the house,
a kind of human Sunday'.[10] It was the familiar pietist situation
of so many creative figures. Patrick's published works include
poems, stories and sermons; his literary ambitions are another
clue to his character. A significant early letter reveals him 'coun-
termanding' the children's intention to cut short a visit to some
friends.[11] He had amateur scientific interests, such as mesmerism
and ballistics.[12] His still somewhat mysterious relationship with
his children seems to have been histrionic as well as didactic, to
judge from the story he told Mrs Gaskell of how he hoped to
draw them out by telling them to speak while wearing a mask.[13]
('Much could not be told', Mrs Gaskell inexplicitly told a friend
after her *Life of Charlotte Brontë* was published, 'of small details
that would have made them understood.'[14]) Emily's recom-
mendation of corporal punishment for her brother on this occasion
is in keeping with one side of her character. The recently discovered diary-notes (for 1834 and 1837) and Charlotte's early
letters make it clear that they were not deprived of the usual extras
and accomplishments in their education at home. They had local
tutors for music and drawing. Ellen Nussey's account of Emily's
musical talent[15] is confirmed by her teaching the younger children
at the pensionnat in Brussels. Miss W. Gérin has recently revealed
further sources of their drawings in books of engravings and early
nineteenth-century Annuals;[16] their imaginations were kindled
by reproductions of Fuseli and John Martin, whose Ossianic rocks
and waterfalls are a pictorial Gondal. Emily copied vignettes

from Thomas Bewick and engravings by William and Edward
Finden from that family source-book, Thomas Moore's *Journals
and Letters of Byron*.[17] Hareton, in *Wuthering Heights*, even before
his reclamation by the younger Catherine 'seemed studying the
familiar landscape with a stranger's and an artist's interest', while
later 'the work they studied was full of costly pictures' (chs. XXI
and XXXII).

One reason, certainly, for the special dominance of the home life
of the Brontës was that it provided scope for the strangest and
richest fantasy-lives recorded of any of the Victorian novelists.
But in this period of romantic influences upon confined and pro-
tracted childhood their imaginings find parallels in the dream-
worlds of De Quincey, Chateaubriand and others. Elizabeth
Barrett, like Charlotte Brontë, was surveying a full writing life
when hardly in her teens.[18] Beatrix Potter kept a secret journal
reminiscent of the Brontës' miniature manuscripts.

The genesis of the dream-worlds, first disclosed when Mrs
Gaskell quoted from their own accounts of it, was in the post-
1825 period. Before Charlotte was fourteen she produced a catalogue of her 'Books up to 1830', which occupies a page and a half
of close print.[19] They all wrote from childhood (with periods of
discouragement and interruption); they produced stories, poems,
translations and drafts of novels. The 'burning clime' of Angria
created by Charlotte and her brother gradually cooled off into a
more realistic Yorkshire or Brussels. The three sisters all show a
relationship – in the works of Charlotte and Emily, especially,
an illuminating one – between their early imaginings and their
novels. Charlotte's 'almond rod' (in the poem 'We wove a web
in childhood') is a symbol of organic development. The early
writing is also a chronicle providing evidence of the family
relationships and culture: 'With what eagerness Papa tore off the
cover', i.e. of the local paper, 'and how we all gathered round him,
and with what breathless anxiety we listened, as one by one they
were disclosed, and explained, and argued upon so ably and so
well . . .'[20] (The topic was the terms for Catholic Emancipation
in 1829.) Charlotte's 'Tales of the Islanders' reveals Emily's early

interest in Scott and Lockhart,[21] and her 'History of the Year
1829' listed the periodicals available to them. Isolated as they
were, *Blackwood's* and *Fraser's* magazines, both of which they saw
regularly, were vital links with a wider intellectual world. They
were especially so for Emily. As editors and contributors to their
own imitations of the reviews, Charlotte and Branwell reproduced
the coterie note of the originals with an Irish talent for mimicry.
The heyday of the periodicals was not consistently an age of
polished style or high seriousness, but, isolated with only a limited
range of English classics, the Brontës escaped or grew out of the
Victorian upholstery and coarse jocularity of the *Blackwood's* circle.
Africa, mother of monsters, was imaginatively colonised by them
through reading the literature of exploration in *Blackwood's* in the
early 1820s.[22] The suspension bridges and wool-combing shops
of the industrial revolution were strangely transferred to this
setting, before Charlotte's Pennine wind of realism blows away
the khamsin. As with all subjective life, the dream-worlds were
both refuge and prison; an invisible vocation that explains their
reactions to real-life situations as revealed, for instance, in Charlotte's pent-up Roe Head diary. Emily's counterpart is a poem
such as 'A little while' (H92) with its complaint at the toil of
institutional life. The artist's burden of living two existences at
once is heavier when one of them is largely an escape. 'Growing
potatoes in a cellar' – Mary Taylor's image for the dream-worlds
is apt,[23] from her own bluff practical point of view, but it must
be remembered that these organisms flowered into daylight.

In 1831 Charlotte went to the Misses Wooler's school, Roe
Head, and her absence probably resulted indirectly in the creation
of a separate imaginary cycle by Emily and Anne. The initiation
of Gondal, that factor which enters so prominently, if not altogether desirably, into any consideration of Emily Brontë, was
possibly a reaction against the temporary leadership of their
brother, motivated by distaste for certain characteristics of the
shared plays, such as moral anarchy and perfunctory violence.
There is no precise record of this inception. The first number of a
juvenile 'publication', the 'Monthly Intelligencer', of which

Branwell was editor, reproves the 'cheif Genii' (Charlotte) for having left his children, who have now attained independence, while a later reference in the same text to rival kingdoms is significant.[24] The best dating of Emily's first known Gondal poem, 'What winter floods' (H96) puts it as early as 1832,[25] which agrees well with these hints, thus indicating an inception of the cycle by this year, or before Emily was fifteen.

Gondal certainly retained vestiges of their shared fantasies. Charlotte's tale 'The Foundling' (1833), combining Pennine place-names with Miltonic descriptions of northern landscape, refers to institutions, such as 'a sort of college or university' similar to the colleges and 'palaces of instruction' of the Gondal poems. The appearance in the same work of a 'Philosopher's Island', with its Gordale mountains, also indicates related material and suggests that 'Gondal' may be an Ossianic version of the local name – another link with the common stuff of European romanticism.[26]

The biographical and historical 'books' mentioned in the birthday and other diary fragments have disappeared. There are a few references to Gondal characters and events, some lists of names and the poetry. 'Like twins', wrote Ellen Nussey of the collaborators, and a gloss in Anne's geography primer merges the real and the fanciful, and is the main evidence for the setting of the Gondal poems. Anne's poems are few and her characters different. Thus almost the whole of the Gondal writing to survive consists of poems by Emily.

'The Gondals are discovering the interior of Gaaldine' – Emily's first laconic reference to the epic, in her note of November 1824, suggests its character. It was a heroic, courtly world based less on reality than on literature. Both its moral and physical geography were austere and northern (an important distinction from Angria); its genetic links with Scott[27] suggest that it reflects the nineteenth-century passion for the north. But the tone and ideology reflect the legacy of romantic literature, modified as she developed by Emily's own outlook. The narrative seems to have been their own invention. The fatal Augusta's relationships with the Heathcliff-like Julius, the troubadour Fernando, and the betrayed, Linton-like Alfred express Emily's peculiar concept of love, which is invariably, at its most intense, involved with hatred and regret (especially for the lost paradise of childhood), as well as her mysticism. The story covered the events of several generations, with a political background showing a certain awareness of social conditions in the Hungry Forties.

No one has succeeded in reconstructing a full and incontrovertible version of the story or stories from the poems and scanty additional evidence. W. D. Paden ends his careful version with the conclusion that it is dangerous to be dogmatic about the details.[28] Other attempts confirm this abundantly. The Gondal frontier is best crossed at mapped points, when they exist, and only when there is good reason to do so.

Gondal seems to have been an instant imaginary universe.

> The Gondal events did not become [W. H. Miller has written] part of a vanished past after they had occurred. They functioned for Emily Brontë just as religious myths functioned for the Greek poets and tragedians. Transformed into a collection of eternal events, they were happening over and over again all the time, always there to be returned to and re-created in poetry. Emily often wrote poems about Gondal events several years after the narrative had, in the sisters' creation of it, reached that stage of its happening . . . In one sense the Gondal saga was a sequence of temporally related events, like history. In another sense it was the simultaneous existence of all its events in a perpetual present . . . [29]

Anyone who tries to follow the story carefully will agree. For instance, there are poems 'by' or about Julius and Augusta written long after their deaths. But the important phrase here is 'They functioned *for Emily Brontë*'. Unlike the works based on the Greek myths, Gondal was not shared with an audience – except of one, and later, apparently, not even this. Emily made no attempt to get her poems published until persuaded by Charlotte to permit it in 1845/6, when certain Gondal poems, isolated, were praised by the critics.

Beginning as a fantasy shared with her younger sister, Gondal was indulged in longer than her siblings' dream-worlds, and though it was not the cause of her isolation – that was her own nature – its character was a product of it. Gondal shows both the peculiarities of her case and some of its strengths. Isolation is both vantage-point and prison. The Gondal writing was not produced under the restraint, the incentive to form and coherence, provided by an audience, but its intensity and singularity spring from the same conditions. In this dramatisation of the inner life can be followed the growth of an imagination, of a cosmos, and an idealised, yet pessimistic conception of human relationships that was extended into *Wuthering Heights*.

It implies a criticism of the Gondal poetry that it is read, despite the incidental rewards, largely as part of the study of the author of a novel, rather than as an assured creation. (The anthology-piece, in the case of 'Silent is the House', is lifted from context.) Much of it is bad or perfunctory, though of course, it is the work of a young writer. Its production by the author of such an assured if slight poem as 'Fall, leaves, fall' (H79) suggests that it was routine stuff, as some indications in the diary-notes confirm.

> Fall, leaves, fall; die, flowers, away;
> Lengthen night and shorten day;
> Every leaf speaks bliss to me
> Fluttering from the autumn tree.
> I shall smile when wreaths of snow
> Blossom where the rose should grow;
> I shall sing when night's decay
> Ushers in a drearier day.

There is nothing, at first sight, remarkable about this, but the ideas cohere delicately, and the mood is singular. The lack of ore, in Keats's sense, in much of Emily's poetry is partly a limitation of her situation. But in *Wuthering Heights* the reluctant novelist had to use the least abstract of forms, and was forced in the direction of life, of concrete experience.

II

THERE are only occasional glimpses of Emily in Charlotte's Nussey correspondence during the early 1830s, when Charlotte was passing on her – for the Brontës – expensive education to her sisters still at home: 'an account of one day is an account of all. In the morning from nine o'clock to half past twelve I instruct my sisters and draw, then we walk till dinner . . .'[1]

Miss Branwell ran the household to a strict routine. Throughout her life Emily is often described, or refers to herself as, variously, brushing carpets, baking, 'turning' and ironing. Like her sisters, she often reproved herself for laziness, but was evidently industrious and efficient.

Ellen Nussey's early visits resulted in the millstone-grit pastoral of her reminiscences of this period: 'Emily, half reclining on a slab of stone, played like a young child with the tadpoles in the water, making them swim about, and then fell to moralising on the strong and the weak.'[2] It is almost too much like the imagined childhood of the author of *Wuthering Heights*, which was published long before Ellen herself was published. At this time Emily evidently revealed (like many heroines of such memoirs) a rather masculine, daring side when out of doors and relaxed: she had also, according to Ellen, a certain magnetism despite her reserve, a charismatic quality, a 'strength of containment seen in no other'. She was a 'law unto herself, and a heroine in keeping to that law'.

This was also the period of the group portrait, which includes the only undisputed portrait of her.[3] (There are several separate drawings and studies of Charlotte and Anne, but the only portraits or putative portraits of Emily are or were parts of groups, which suggests that, as with publication, she would join in, but preferred to remain out of sight if possible.) The famous group was painted before Branwell's promise had faded; indeed before his undoubted talent had developed. 'Little better than sign-painting,' wrote Mrs Gaskell of this 'pillar' portrait, while conceding that the likeness of Charlotte – the only sister she actually met – was excellent.

This Branwell primitive is interesting for its individual characterisation, and in its evocation of a certain stress and aspiration in its young subjects. This, one feels, is the Brontës as they lived: Emily with the 'tight, unbecoming hair style', that Ellen Nussey mentions, looks out this once as she was 'quelque chose de rêveur et de souffrant', with her companion Anne's head almost on her shoulder. Her eyes are wide-set, her face rather small and triangular, indicating through its likeness to an early portrait of her father that perhaps she took after him. Her appearance here also confirms the likeness to G. H. Lewes at which Charlotte later exclaimed.[4] Then there is the fictional Shirley, who nevertheless rather resembles the Emily of the group portrait: 'Her features were distinguished, by which I do not mean that they were high, bony and Roman, being indeed rather small and slightly marked than otherwise.'[5] 'Emily's countenance', wrote Mrs Gaskell – she had seen the portrait – 'struck me as full of power.' Ellen Nussey described her eyes as 'dark gray, at other times dark blue', but 'she did not often look at you'. Her glance was 'something to remember through life'.

There is first-hand evidence of the circumstances of writing and, to some extent, of the sources of many Victorian novels, such as *Dombey and Son* and *Middlemarch*. That this is not so of *Wuthering Heights*, plus its unusual artistic character, lends a certain interest to such evidence as there is for Emily Brontë's reading and tastes. For the sisters we have Charlotte's well-known reading list in a letter of 1834,[6] recommending Shakespeare's tragedies and histories, Byron's *Don Juan* and *Cain*, Milton, Goldsmith, Pope, Scott, Wordsworth and Southey, as well as some standard lives – Southey's *Nelson*, Lockhart's *Burns* and Moore's *Byron*. It was an eclectic product of the experience of her Roe Head education, their

own modest library and the now celebrated Keighley Mechanics'
Institute library, which their father had joined. (When Mrs
Gaskell first visited the parsonage in 1853 the few books she
saw in Mr Brontë's study bring to mind the meagre parsonage
reading that wearied Caroline Helstone in *Shirley*, but in the
parlour, presided over by Charlotte, there were 'two recesses, on
each side of the high, narrow, old-fashioned mantel-piece, filled
with books'.[7] By then, of course, Charlotte had many literary
acquaintances.)

The Brontës' works as a whole, and the internal clues in Emily's
own, confirm that certain writers in Charlotte's 1834 list –
Shakespeare, Scott, Wordsworth, Byron and Moore on Byron –
were important to her development, but there is a dark side to the
moon. What fiction other than Scott's influenced *Wuthering Heights*
and what romantic ideologies, if any? Emily's attitudes to literature seem to have been conflicting (if the hints in *Wuthering
Heights* are any guide): books were dead, bourgeois, stifling, the
refuge of characters inadequate to the element of high passion and
feeling, but they were also an important factor in the main-
tenance of civilisation, in the ordinary process of life. As might
be expected, few of her books have been found. But she was
socially the most isolated, intellectually the most gifted, of a
family with an exceptional dependence on the printed word. It is
understandable that there should be a close connection between
her writing and the mythology deriving from the works – and the
lives – of the great romantics of the previous generation. In this
she is, perhaps, a special case. The fact may justify some indulgence in the second-rate activity of tracing it. (The regional grain
in *Wuthering Heights* must not be underrated either.) An apparent
affinity in *Wuthering Heights* with the ideas of Spinoza or Shelley
doesn't imply she had read them. Sensitiveness to (in Charlotte's
phrase) 'daring and original beliefs' through the medium of
commentary and criticism seems to have played an important part.

A descendant of the Heaton family of Ponden House, about two
miles from Haworth, later wrote – there is no corroborative
evidence – that Emily was the only member of the Brontë family
friendly with them.[8] ('Intercourse with them she never sought',

Charlotte wrote of her relations with the local people, 'or with very rare exceptions ever experienced.') Mrs Gaskell referred to the intransigent local families – this one possessed a library of over 1300 books, including a First Folio; much seventeenth- and eighteenth-century poetry – Crashaw, Cleveland, Akenside, Cowley and Gray – but few nineteenth-century works of any kind, or works related to romanticism. But it could have provided the law books, written for laymen, such as Runnington's *Ejectment*, and Lovelass's *The Laws Disposing of a Person's Estate*, needed for Emily Brontë's occult knowledge of property law in *Wuthering Heights*. This possible connection was never mentioned on the Brontës' side (nor, perhaps for reasons of family dignity, was the Mechanics' Institute), but Miss Gérin claims to have established it on internal evidence.[9] The question remains controversial. Charlotte stated fairly definitely that her sister's contacts with Haworth life were mainly at second hand, for instance via the old servant 'Tabby', Tabitha Aykroyd, whom they liked. On the other hand, one suspects her of a tendency to exaggerate her sisters' seclusion and dependence.

It is justifiable to consider Emily against their collective literary background when considering the influence of De Quincey. There are obvious similarities between his timidity and sense of doom, his precocious childhood scarred by early bereavement, and theirs. They found some deeply felt experience reflected in the work of one of the most brilliant writers of their period. Charlotte acknowledged the 'pleasure and profit' they owed him when presenting him with a copy of the 1846 volume of poems.[10] The connection is most obvious in the occasional 'mode of impassioned prose' (his own phrase) of Charlotte's novels, probably influenced by Carlyle also (though Charlotte wrote she did not like him) and in Branwell's life and writing, which both indicate his influence. This mode is not found in the cooler, more restrained prose of *Wuthering Heights*, though the tender nerve of Emily's poem 'Stars' is in a sector of experience explored by De Quincey. Both Branwell's and Charlotte's work suggest a familiarity with the celebrated 'Suspiria de Profundis', published in *Blackwood's* in 1845. De Quincey's intermittent contributions to

Blackwood's coincide almost exactly with the life-span of the Brontës.

G. D. Klingopulos has defined the elements that are relevant.

> Though he lacked the moral concentration and ability to sim-
> plify that go to make a novelist, he was interested in the power
> of language to express modes of consciousness that not even
> poetry could adequately render; the experience of dreams and
> music, the impressions of childhood, the arrest of time under
> the influence of laudanum, the sense of multitude and tumult
> and fear; and he had the confidence of genius in the originality
> of his mode of autobiography, his vision of his own life. His
> nature was that of a lifelong younger brother, too unassertive,
> rather feminine, sensual, but with its own integrity.[11]

The Brontës evidently responded to his work, singling it out from the mass of often coarse and ephemeral periodical writing for the qualities that have given their own, classic status – sensibility and psychological truth. He was a pioneer in the subjectivism that is part of their originality. His contributions on German literature (though they did not all appear in *Blackwood's*) should dispel any idea that the Brontës were necessarily cut off from such a European influence. The relationship needs more detailed study. Of course De Quincey is in a different category to the Brontës: he was more versatile, important as an essayist, not without interest as a historian, and original as critic; he was in touch with the culture of the period in depth in a way they could hardly be. They knew few things, passion and isolation among them, but De Quincey knew many things. Charlotte, however, certainly knew the melancholia for which he provided a kind of mythology.

The abrupt end of the second attempt to give Emily a normal education, as explained by her sister in her 'Preface to the Literary Remains of Emily and Anne Brontë' in the 1850 edition of *Wuthering Heights*, seems entirely predictable in view of her sensitivity and love of freedom. In all probability it was homesickness so acute that it threatened her health that led to her removal from Roe Head in 1835. Yet Charlotte's account is so linked with anomalies in her presentation of the other evidence, the poems, and with her omission of any mention of Law Hill, Halifax (itself a biographical problem), that one cannot but scrutinise it carefully.

Emily accompanied her as pupil to Roe Head when Charlotte returned as teacher on 29 July 1835 (the day before Emily's seventeenth birthday).[12] Within three months she was at home again, her place taken by Anne. Charlotte's account is a convincing description of her love of liberty, of her need for that 'very noiseless, very secluded' but unrestricted and inartificial mode of life' that is the familiar pattern of her existence.

> Liberty was the breath of Emily's nostrils; without it, she perished. The change from her own home to a school, and from her own very noiseless, very secluded, but unrestricted and in-artificial mode of life, to one of disciplined routine (though under the kindest auspices), was what she failed in enduring. Her nature proved here too strong for her fortitude. Every morning when she woke, the vision of home and the moors rushed upon her, and darkened and saddened the day that lay before her. Nobody knew what ailed her but me – I knew only too well. In this struggle her health was quickly broken; her white face, attenuated form, and failing strength, threatened rapid decline. I felt in my heart she would die, if she did not go home, and with this conviction obtained her recall.

(The atmosphere of the mode of life to which Charlotte refers is conveyed by the first of Emily's diary papers, of 24 November 1834, a few months before. It begins: 'I fed Rainbow, Diamond Snowflake, Jasper phaesent (alias) this morning . . .'[13] The throwaway style and list of pets suggests that the model for the diary-notes was Byron's *Journal*, from the extracts used by Moore. Compare 'Fed the two cats, the hawk, and the tame (but not *tamed*) crow . . .' 6 January 1821.)[14]

The Preface quoted, which continues with an account of Brussels and Emily's successful struggle against homesickness there, is the only summary of her sister's life left by Charlotte. She does not mention that Emily not only became a teacher after her failure as a pupil, but was, in all probability, a successful one, for over a year. She went to Miss Patchett's school, Law Hill, Halifax, two years after Roe Head, in the autumn of 1837.

The gist of this problem, which is not irrelevant to Emily's character and experience, and the experience that went into *Wuthering Heights*, is as follows: Mrs Gaskell, on the authority not of Charlotte herself, but of Ellen Nussey alone, stated in *The Life of Charlotte Brontë* that Emily was at Law Hill for only six months. But one of her poems, 'A little while' (H92), describes the stresses of being a teacher, is a 'personal' poem, and is dated December 1838, or fourteen months after she went to the school. This poem was chosen from Emily's manuscripts by Charlotte for publication in 1850 and is altered so that it reads as if written by a pupil, in other words to illustrate Charlotte's account of her sister at Roe Head. It is introduced by her as a Roe Head poem though no such poems exist.

It is easy to exaggerate the importance of this kind of problem. It is not clear whether Charlotte, writing many years later, simply forgot that her sister had been to Law Hill, or did not think it worth mentioning; or whether, when she presented the Law Hill poem (or, at any rate, certainly *not* Roe Head poem) as a pupil's poem, she knew where it had been written or just did not look at the date; or whether, believing it to be a Roe Head poem, her alteration of the stanza to read from a pupil's standpoint rather than a teacher's ('the noisy crowd are barred away' becomes 'the weary task is put away') was in order not to offend the surviving headmistress, Miss Wooler; or for the less-justifiable reason of concealing the fact that her sister had been to Law Hill.

It seems at least possible that Charlotte was guilty of some manipulation of the evidence here. This is perhaps not the only instance of her presenting her sisters as more dependent than they in fact were. Charlotte had a powerful, photographic memory, and it seems unlikely that she could have forgotten that her sister went to Law Hill. The omission throws a certain suspicion on her account of what happened at Roe Head also. It would, perhaps, be going too far to suggest that there was more to it than home-sickness. The change from her previous life, to one of disciplined routine, was what she failed in enduring,[15] she wrote of this time, when Emily was in effect her pupil, in the difficult position of second sister to another strong character, who had had senior sisterhood thrust upon her. On the other hand, rebellious feelings against institutional restraints were, perhaps, to be expected from the creator-to-be of the young Heathcliff and Catherine.

The circumstances at the time of writing of Charlotte's Preface suggest a possible motive. It was in 1849, soon after Emily's death, and was a commission from Smith, Elder, who were to republish *Wuthering Heights* with *Agnes Grey* and some poems. The task was welcome as a therapy for her own unhappiness, but it was a costly therapy in terms of the misery it re-awoke. The poems Charlotte edited evidently added to her understanding of her sister. 'Nobody knew what ailed her but me' – only a few months before she wrote this account of events fourteen years earlier, she had for the second time known only too well what ailed her sister, but her offer of aid had been refused. Perhaps the Preface can be read as influenced by a desire to do in print for the sister whose confidence she did not possess what was not permitted in life.

'Every morning when she woke', Charlotte wrote of Roe Head, 'the vision of home and the moors rushed upon her.' (Such waking sorrows had been described by De Quincey.) In the account of Catherine Earnshaw's illness (*Wuthering Heights*, ch. XII), in which she tells Nelly Dean of her grief after separation from Heathcliff,

> But, supposing at twelve years old I had been wrenched from the Heights, and every early association, and my all in all, as Heathcliff was at that time, and been converted at a stroke into Mrs Linton, the lady of Thrushcross Grange, and the wife of a stranger; an exile, and outcast, thenceforth, from what had been my world – You may fancy a glimpse of the abyss where I grovelled!

there is, perhaps, a *transposition d'art* of the Roe Head incident and thus a confirmation of it as Charlotte presents it.

After the release from Roe Head, at a time when her brother and sisters too were busily writing, Emily – on the evidence of her

manuscripts – applied herself intensely to poetry. One, at least, of
the early poems 'I am the only being whose doom' (H11) goes
some way towards providing a rationale of the withdrawal. These
Gondal imprisonments and liberations, these hauntings by alien
powers, may reflect a conflict between intimations of damnation
and of immortality – in Calvin-tinged Evangelicalism and in
nature respectively. At times, as with 'I saw thee, child, one
summer's day' (H14), they suggest the confrontation between
Emily Brontë's everyday self and her creative impulse. Though
some of them are less deeply felt exercises in the manner of Byron,
Coleridge (in *Christabel*) and Wordsworth, they anticipate themes
and characteristics of better poems to come.

Scott, to be felt in the 'shining and lowering and swelling and
dying' of a fragment (H5) of December 1836, is soon supplanted
in the Gondal poems by Byron, much as he was in the taste of the
period. Emily Brontë is a first choice to exemplify his pervasive
influence on nineteenth-century poetry. It affected her to such an
extent that the question occurs whether she has a poetic identity.
It can be satisfactorily answered by the later works.

These early, anonymous, but often, certainly, Gondal poems
reflect Byron's lyrics ('There shines the moon, at noon of night'
– H9) or the festal-elegiac manner of the Waterloo part of *Childe
Harold*.

> Through the hours of yesternight
> Hall and gallery blazed with light;
> Every lamp its lustre showered
> On the adorer and the adored.
> None were sad that entered there,
> All were loved, and all were fair . . .   (H8)

The greatest Byron, the masculine satiric energy and individual
feeling of *Beppo* and *Don Juan* (competently imitated by Charlotte
in her juvenilia), was neglected by her sister in favour of the
'Byronism' of the Oriental Tales.

> No – there was something in his face,
> Some nameless thing they could not trace . . .
> Youthful he seemed – but worn as they   (H107)

'I am the only being whose doom' (H11) is more revealing as a statement of romantic pessimism and misanthropy. Dated 17 May 1837, it shows no particular indication of being a Gondal poem and in the words 'As friendless after eighteen years' alludes to her actual age. (This preoccupation with time as a scale to measure the force of feeling by, persisted with Emily Brontë. It seems to be characteristic of the working of her mind. One recalls the precise chronology of *Wuthering Heights*: 'Cold in the earth, and *fifteen* wild Decembers'; Catherine's 'I've been a waif for *twenty* years'; 'it was the same room into which he [Heathcliff] had been ushered as a guest, *eighteen* years before'.) The poem reveals moments of weakness when Byronism is abandoned and the standpoint of the outcast sounds rather half-hearted; one senses the claims on the Brontës of normal life.

> There have been times I cannot hide,
> There have been times when this was drear,
> When my sad soul forgot its pride
> And longed for one to love me here.
>
> But those were in the early glow
> Of feelings since subdued by care;
> And they have died so long ago,
> I hardly now believe they were. (H11)

The latter stanza is a paraphrase of Scott's review of Canto III of *Childe Harold* in the *Quarterly Review*, October 1816: 'The strength of early passion and the glow of youthful feeling, are uniformly painted as chilled or subdued by a train of early imprudences or of darker guilt . . .' Some back issues of the *Quarterly Review* were stocked by the local library,[16] but Emily Brontë may have seen a quotation of the review. Scott is defining the Byronic, or what came to be called the Byronic, man, and goes on to discuss his creator's identification with him. The impression evidently made on her by his commentary on Byron suggests no passing interest. Poetry is not produced by detached copying of models. Emily's early poems are slight, as might be expected, but they are not merely exercises. She calls in Byron to redress a genuine personal predicament.

'Twas grief enough to think mankind
All hollow, servile, insincere;
But worse to trust to my own mind
And find the same corruption there.

This is not Byronism, but Puritanism. The hollow, servile
humanity here anticipates the 'Foot-kissers of triumphant crime'
of her last, socially conscious, poem. The Brussels *devoirs* will
provide more direct evidence of her reflection about human
nature.

Philip Henderson has aptly compared the chiaroscuro of some
of these early poems to Victorian steel-engravings.[17]

The smothering snow-clouds rolled away;
And cold – how cold! – wan moonlight smiled
Where those black ruins smouldering lay.   (H29)

Frequent echoes of Wordsworth, Coleridge and Cowper reveal
the forces making for a common, derivative, post-romantic
Zeitgeist.

And far beyond the sparkling trees
Of the castle park, one sees
The bare heath spreading clear as day
Moor behind moor, far far away . . .

These 'Gondal' lines, which might have come from Emily
Brontë's 'To A.G.A.' or 'Written in Aspin Castle', neither of
which was published during the nineteenth century, are by
Matthew Arnold (*Tristram and Iseult*, 1852).

A poem such as 'I saw thee, child' (H14) of July 1837 seems to
reflect the contemporary debate about Calvinism as well as
Wordsworth's 'Immortality' ode.

Poor child, if spirits such as I
Could weep o'er human misery,
A tear might flow, aye, many a tear,
To see the road that lies before,
To see the sunshine disappear,
And hear the stormy waters roar,
Breaking upon a desolate shore,
Cut off from hope in early day,
From power and glory cut away.

This poem, like 'The night of storms has passed' (H12) and 'O God of heaven!' (H15), contains no direct indication that it is a Gondal poem, but though these situations are evidently fictional, as might be expected, their content is not. The lines in 'I saw thee, child',

> You longed for fate to raise the veil
> That darkened over coming years . . .

echo the end of Emily Brontë's prose note, written on her brother's birthday, 26 June 1837, the month before that in which the poem is dated. This detailed, informal, domestic chronicle, in which the real and the imaginary come literally in the same breath ('Tabby in the kitchin – the Emperors and Empresses of Gondal and Gaaldine preparing to depart from Gaaldine to Gondal for the coronation'[18]) looks ahead to the end of another four-year period, like the later notes: 'I wonder where we shall be and how we shall be and what kind of a day it will be then let us hope for the best.' 'The night of storms is passed' is listed by Hatfield as two poems (H12 and 13), but is clearly one, a description of a dream visitation followed by a choric lament.

> O bring not back again
> The horror of that hour
> When its lips opened, and a sound
> Awoke the stillness reigning round . . .
>
> 'Woe for the day; Regina's pride,
> Regina's hope is in the grave . . .

This spectral lament, in the poem of 10 June 1837, was evidently connected with an assassination at the coronation mentioned in the prose note of 26 June. (Such an event is the subject of 'Gleneden's Dream' of a year later.)

It is tempting to link a poem such as 'O God of heaven! the dream of horror', with its reference to a release from prison, with the Calvinist atmosphere of the Clergy Daughters' School.

> The impatient rage, the useless shrinking
> From thoughts that yet could not be borne;
> The soul that was for ever thinking,
> Till nature, maddened, tortured, sinking,
> At last refused to mourn –

It's over now – and I am free,
And the ocean wind is caressing me,
The wild wind from that wavy main
I never thought to see again.

Bless thee, Bright Sea – and glorious dome,
And my own world, my spirit's home . . .

There is nevertheless a striking similarity between this poem and
a passage in Cowper's *Memoir*, in which he describes a sudden
relief of his melancholia that had the abruptness and force of an
ecstatic experience.

the morning was mild and serene, the sun shone brightly on the
sea, and the country upon the borders of it was the most beautiful I had ever seen. We sat down upon an eminence at the end
of the arm of the sea which is between Southampton and the
New Forest. Here it was that, on a sudden, as if another sun had
been kindled that instant in the heavens, on purpose to dispel
sorrow and vexation of spirit, I felt all the weight of misery
taken off; my heart became light and joyful in a moment. I
could have wept with transport had I been alone. I must needs
believe that nothing but the almighty could have filled me with
such an inexpressible delight; not by a gradual dawning of
peace, but, as it were, with a flash of his life giving countenance.[19]

(There is also a similarity between this passage and later poems by
Emily Brontë.) Here she may very well be interpreting experience
in terms of literature. Cowper's orthodox explanation of the
experience is not accepted; as with Catherine Earnshaw in
Wuthering Heights, it is 'my own world, my spirit's home' that
heals the agony

of still repining,
When not a spark of hope was shining
From gloomy fate's relentless sky . . .

Both Mrs Gaskell and Mary Taylor testified to the Brontës'
familiarity with Cowper,[20] the former also to the kinship of
experience between them. Emily need not have seen the above

passage in an edition of Cowper; it was quoted in the issue of the *Quarterly Review* containing Scott's review of Byron already referred to.

To consider, finally, another poem of the period, the simple, revealing statement of the evidently more autobiographical 'Alone I sat; the summer day' (H27) shows little justification for her self-doubt in face of the promptings of the imagination.

> Alone I sat; the summer day
> Had died in smiling light away;
> I saw it die, I watched it fade
> From misty hill and breezeless glade;
>
> And thoughts in my soul were gushing,
> And my heart bowed beneath their power;
> And tears within my eyes were rushing
> Because I could not speak the feeling,
> The solemn joy around me stealing
> In that divine, untroubled hour.

This shows a relationship with the later, more powerful ecstatic poems, and gives a clue to what they are about.

III

THE 'Law Hill problem' has been mentioned above. In her June 1837 diary-note Emily Brontë did not refer to the prospect of going out as a teacher. The offer may have arisen suddenly, perhaps via her brother, who was himself attempting to become established as a painter in near-by Bradford. The first that is heard of her at school is in a letter from Charlotte to Ellen Nussey in the autumn of 1837. Its exact date is uncertain, but it was probably October. Charlotte mentions having heard from Emily once, adding that she was now in a large school and that her account gave grounds for anxiety about her health. 'Hard labour from six in the morning until near eleven at night, with only one half-hour of exercise in between . . . I fear she will never stand it.'[1] After this, Emily disappears from the records (except for a single allusion to 'my sisters' by Charlotte in mid-1838,[2] which gives no indication of whether she was still employed) until the middle of 1839, when she was evidently living at home once more.

The absence of any further account of this period from Emily herself is not compensated for by reports from others. As an obscure young teacher of nineteen, the only impression she made is contained in recollections of some pupils which E. A. Chadwick claimed to have obtained after 1900, and which have become part of the apocrypha.[3] But if the relationships of the period are an almost total blank, its background still exists or can be reconstructed, and has inevitably been investigated, providing fairly convincing evidence of its contribution to the experience that helped to form *Wuthering Heights*.

Law Hill, in the Southowram district of Halifax, is a property consisting of a small group of late-eighteenth-century buildings on Beacon Hill, now an extremity of one of the city's climbing hill-suburbs. It includes farm buildings, Law Hill house, and a warehouse, the group enclosing a courtyard, and suggesting a characteristic West Riding unit of the period before the textile industry was concentrated in factories. The district is still not fully built over, and the garden of Law Hill adjoins open high farm land, resembling moor. The history of Law Hill may be reflected in a minor way in *Wuthering Heights*: the topography of the district is a stronger claimant.

The original owner, for whom the house was built, was a Halifax character whose story is described in the diary[4] of a member of the family he exploited. Taken into their household as dependent nephew, he was clever and unscrupulous enough to gain control of their business. Heathcliff, to the extent that he is a villain of property melodrama (but no more), may owe something to this man. Curiously enough Charlotte, when referring in her Preface (1850) to Emily's tendency to select 'those tragic and terrible traits of which, in listening to the secret annals of every rude vicinage, the memory is sometimes compelled to receive the impress', was describing her seclusion at home.

Early in the nineteenth century Law Hill was bought by the Misses Maria and Elizabeth Patchett and became a school. Maria died in 1835. Elizabeth had a staff of two assistant teachers and four servants. There were twenty boarders, aged between eleven and fifteen, at the time of the 1841 census.[5] On 27 December 1842 Miss Patchett married the incumbent of her parish, and retired, and Law Hill was advertised for sale.[6] She was evidently a good business-woman, well known in the district, and of some cultivation.

According to tradition the schoolroom, the 'naked room' of Emily's poem 'A little while', was in the adjoining outbuilding. The number of pupils supports this tradition. Mrs Chadwick wrote that she had seen correspondence written by a former pupil who remembered Emily Brontë during the winter of 1838-9.[7] This informant described Emily's 'devotion to the house-dog which she once told her pupils was dearer to her than they were'. The story seems true to the character of the woman who wrote 'The Cat'. Mrs Chadwick also discovered, she claimed, that Miss

Patchett encouraged her pupils to take an interest in the amenities of Halifax, which were considerable for the period, and in its topography, but she provides no references.[8]

The landscape and architecture of the Law Hill district certainly made an impression on one of them. Hardy, a more naturalistic novelist than Emily, called his landscapes 'partly real, partly dream',[9] which was also true of Emily's. The search for Brontë originals can be tedious, and the fact that when she wrote *Wuthering Heights* she drew to some extent on a remembered landscape is less interesting than that this landscape, in which she lived for such a limited period, imposed itself on country she had known intimately throughout her life. Students of Emily Brontë have known, at least from the 1920s, that the grotesque main gateway of the now-vanished High Sunderland, a Jacobean moorland landowner's house that stood on high ground just outside the city, was so much to the romantic taste (literary rather than architectural Gothic) that Lockwood's first impressions of Wuthering Heights reproduce it fairly closely.[10] It has also long been known that an engraving of it forms the frontispiece to Horner's *Views of Buildings in the Town and Parish of Halifax* (1835), a work in which Miss Patchett is listed as a subscriber.

There are certain other fairly convincing connections demonstrable between the country on this side of Halifax and the landscape in *Wuthering Heights*. They throw some light on Emily Brontë's still little-known creative processes. There are two notable houses in the area: the second, which survives, is Shibden, a richly detailed stone and timber building in a park on lower ground nearer Law Hill. There are close parallels between the disposition of High Sunderland and Shibden, the features of the area, and the novel (such as the walled park of Shibden, the beck that crosses the area between them, and the vanished 'Chapel-en-le-brier' – from which the name of the church near Law Hill, St Anne's in the Grove, was taken – the probable original of 'Gimmerden Chapel' in the novel, the marsh 'Gimmerden Sough', etc.: 'Gimmerden' and 'Shibden' are semantically related). A map of the area resembles the kind of map that can be drawn from a close reading of the book.[11]

The often used word 'background' is not very appropriate to *Wuthering Heights*, in which description is never used for its own sake, or to provide documentation, but always relevantly to the dramatic texture. This created landscape, both as presented in the novel and figuratively, is a long way from Halifax. Emily Brontë seems to have used those aspects of the Halifax landscape she required, combining them with general and particular details of the country nearer home. (There were no such impressive houses in the Haworth district.) The fusion of details of both the Halifax and Haworth localities in the novel indicates a creative freedom from slavish use of source-material that is very much in accord with the general nature of the work. One possible clue to the process may be pointed out, not with certainty, but for what it is worth. The owner of Shibden in the 1830s was a Miss Lister. Ponden House, near Haworth, traditionally an original of Thrushcross Grange, is sited more in accord with the spirit of the novel than Shibden and probably provided certain details of both houses in *Wuthering Heights*. Its owners were called Heaton. Lister+Heaton=(approximately) Linton.

The dominance of Brussels in Charlotte's novels is not an exact parallel to the striking residue of Halifax in her sister's, but it provides an interesting indication of the mechanism behind the anomaly. Emily, as a 'provincial', was imaginatively receptive when coping with new and strange circumstances on her own.

Emily Brontë also produced a fairly steady output of poetry during both the undisputed and disputed periods at Law Hill. The crucial poem 'A little while' (H92), dated 4 December 1838, is one of a group of meditative 'personal' poems written – or, at any rate, dated – within a few days of each other. They express a characteristic dualist response to contrast. The death of nature is a kind of exile, but

> . . . my heart loves December's smile
> As much as July's golden beam . . .   (H93)

The poems are allusive, their full circumstances are not released, and the result is a certain obscurity, though the moods are well

defined. (It is no wonder there has been a good deal of speculation as to their relationship to her circumstances.)

In the 'school' poem, the general drift, 'home thoughts from
school', is clear enough.

> A little while, a little while,
> The noisy crowd are barred away;
> And I can sing and I can smile
> A little while I've holyday!

After asking 'Where wilt thou go, my harassed heart?' she gives
a well-known evocation of her home.

> There is a spot 'mid barren hills
> Where winter howls and driving rain,
> But if the dreary tempest chills
> There is a light that warms again.
>
> The house is old, the trees are bare
> And moonless bends the misty dome
> But what on earth is half so dear,
> So longed for as the hearth of home?

She continues:

> Shall I go there? or shall I seek
> Another clime, another sky,
> Where tongues familiar music speak
> In accents dear to memory?
>
> Yes, as I mused, the naked room,
> The flickering firelight died away
> And from the midst of cheerless gloom
> I passed to bright, unclouded day—
>
> A little and a lone green lane
> That opened on a common wide;
> A distant, dreamy, dim blue chain
> Of mountains circling every side . . .

But if the choice, as one supposes, is between Gondal ('another
clime') and Haworth, the 'Yes' is not a very direct introduction

to the – as one takes it to be – further description of Haworth. This heavy-handed examination of a pleasing poem is only to show that something gets between Emily Brontë and the communication of outward circumstances. This is one of her most detailed poems, but the school situation is only suggested by 'noisy crowd', 'naked room', 'flickering firelight', etc. After what is perhaps an echo of Herbert's 'Vertue',

> A heaven so clear, an earth so calm,
> So sweet, so soft, so hushed an air
> And, deepening still the dream-like charm,
> Wild moor-sheep feeding everywhere–

there is a return to the anonymous schoolroom.

> I hear my dungeon bars recoil –

No more forthcoming is 'The blue bell is the sweetest flower' (H94) entitled 'The Bluebell' by Charlotte in the 1850 selection. It also suggests the exile theme.

> The blue bell is the sweetest flower
> That waves in summer air;
> Its blossoms have the mightiest power
> To soothe my spirit's care.
>
> There is a spell in purple heath
> Too wildly, sadly dear;
> The violet has a fragrant breath
> But fragrance will not cheer.
>
> The trees are bare, the sun is cold,
> And seldom, seldom seen;
> The heavens have lost their zone of gold
> And earth its robe of green;
>
> And ice upon the glancing stream
> Has cast its sombre shade
> And distant hills and valleys seem
> In frozen mists arrayed.

The blue bell cannot charm me now,
The heath has lost its bloom,
The violets in the glen below
They yield no sweet perfume.

But though I mourn the heather-bell
'Tis better far, away;
I know how fast my tears would swell
To see it smile to-day;

The argument appears to be that the bluebell is the pleasantest
flower to remember when exiled from summer, because the heath,
or heather (which also, confusingly, has blue bells), has associations that are too painful. After the stanzas quoted there follows
a repetition of the whole posy by description, not by name – no
names no pack drill is here a firm principle – in order to confirm
the initial choice. The violet, for instance, is alluded to by what
may be an echo of Wordsworth.

And that wood flower that hides so shy
Beneath its mossy stone
Its balmy scent and dewy eye:
'Tis not for them I moan.

The last stanza seems to clinch the connection between the exile
of the seasons and exile from home.

How do I yearn, how do I pine
For the time of flowers to come,
And turn me from that fading shine
To mourn the fields of home.

These poems show the development of the response to nature
that is dramatised in *Wuthering Heights*.

How still, how happy! Those are words
That once would scarce agree together;
I loved the plashing of the surge . . .

Now I feel
Where silence dwells is sweeter far   (H93)

There is also a direct transcription of the sensibility that is 'modern' and that shows how Emily escaped the worn formalities of much early-nineteenth-century poetry by women. For instance, in 'The blue bell', the lines

> If chilly then the light should fall
> Adown the dreary sky
> And gild the dank and darkened wall
> With transient brilliancy,

anticipate Nelly Dean at the wayside guide post ('The sun shone yellow on its grey head, reminding me of summer', ch. XI). In these unassuming poems Emily Brontë is concentrating on an inner experience rather than a report, so their value to the biographer is perhaps irrelevant. It is worth mentioning, nevertheless, that there is a close agreement between the weather described in 'How still, how happy!' and 'The blue bell' and the real weather, as recorded by a local meteorologist on the dates 4 and 18 December 1838, respectively, of the two poems.[12]

A fragment on a work-sheet of this period, dated June 1838,

> Lonely at her window sitting,
> While the evening stole away;
> Fitful winds, foreboding, flitting
> Through a sky of cloudy grey.   (H66)

suggests a reading of the 1830 Tennyson, which contains *Mariana*. (In 1848 Charlotte bought in London a copy of *The Princess* for Emily, and the interest thus indicated may have commenced at this time.) There were also Gondal poems: the Rider Haggard tree-and-chasm incident in the Gondal ballad 'Douglas's Ride' (H75) recalls the defences of the outcast Balfour, in the Black Linn, in *Old Mortality*, its probable source.[13] 'Light up thy halls!' (H85) is written in a manner in total contrast to that of the personal poems but one also related to Wuthering Heights.

> *Life* bows to my control, but *Love* I cannot kill!

It is the Heathcliff style, though in *Wuthering Heights* it has developed to paradox (cf. 'I can love *my* murderer, but *yours*, never'). It is a somewhat strident poem, but it contains its own moderator – 'vain words, vain frenzied thoughts' and even has a characteristic irreverent wit.

And then I go to prove if God, at least, be true!

To return briefly to the 'Law Hill problem'. The various aspects of this are somewhat complex, involving such questions as the dating of the correspondence, and whether Emily Brontë might have written a poem about school many months after she had left. But it reduces itself to a contradiction between the late 1838 poem 'A little while' and Mrs Gaskell's statement in the *Life* that Emily was at Miss Patchett's school for six months only. She obtained this information from Ellen Nussey, the correspondence being available. (None of the Brontës' contemporaries contradicted it when the *Life* was published.) The fact that Mrs Gaskell did *not* obtain it from Charlotte Brontë herself is significant. It is just possible that Ellen, wanting to refresh her memory of what happened more than fifteen years earlier, turned to Charlotte's 1850 'Preface to the Literary Remains'. 'Her previous life, with the exception of a single half-year, had been passed in the absolute retirement of a village parsonage . . .', i.e. her life previous to her brief attendance at Roe Head, the 'single half-year' referring to Cowan Bridge. Did Ellen misread this as a reference to Law Hill, understandably, since Charlotte Brontë omits this episode altogether from the biographical Preface?

Emily Brontë returned from her Halifax post to three years of austere seclusion at home. By the middle of 1839 the correspondence shows that she was there to undertake some domestic commissions for Charlotte, who was away working as a governess with the Sidgwick family.

Dearest Lavinia [This may have been an allusion to some long-lost character in a silver-fork novel] – I am most exceedingly obliged to you for all the trouble you have taken in seeking up my things and sending them all right. The box and its contents were most acceptable. I only wish I had asked you to send me some letter-paper. This is my last sheet but two. When you

can send the other articles of raiment now manufacturing, I shall
be right down glad of them.[14]

Emily had evidently been able to force herself to endure a
teacher's life this once for a substantial period, but the desired
pattern of her existence was unchanged. (As mentioned, she had
at Halifax surroundings similar to those of Haworth.) In 1848
Charlotte described her sister's temperament to Dr Epps, calling
it 'highly nervous'. Spiritual response to place is closely connected
with health and that, in turn, with a particular way of life.

So her sister Anne's comment is the only appropriate summary
of her external life during 1839 to 1842, during which all the
rest of the Brontë children took situations of one kind or another.
'We are all doing something for our livelihood except Emily, who
is, however, as busy as any of us, and earns her food and raiment
as much as we do.'[15]

'The Gondals still flourish bright as ever', she wrote in 1845,
but before Brussels there is a tendency towards more direct
expression of her ideas and experience, indicating intellectual
development. Lockwood, it will be remembered, misguidedly
visited Wuthering Heights for company, and in her private
poems his creator did not always suppress her loneliness, that
recurrent Brontë theme. In early April 1839 Anne, like her
heroine *Agnes Grey*, went as governess to a family near Mirfield.
Emily's poem 'By R. Gleneden' (H97) seems to reflect the event,
while 'Fair sinks the summer evening now' is a more open poem
of solitude written when Charlotte also was away.

> Then why is all so sad and lone?
> No merry foot-step on the stair –
> No laugh – no heart-awaking tone,
> But voiceless silence everywhere.   (H116)

Another element of Lockwood appears to derive from this
period. The attractive young curate William Weightman was at
Haworth from August 1839 until his death in 1842. His private
life came in for a good deal of comment from Charlotte: 'I am
afraid', she wrote to Ellen Nussey, 'he is very fickle – not to you
in particular, but to half a dozen other ladies, he has just cut his

enamorata at Swansea, and sent her back all her letters . . .'[16]
Lockwood's retreat from an affair at the seaside (*Wuthering Heights*,
ch. 1) emphasises his timidity, and throws into relief the huge
commitment of the protagonists.

The world is not entirely excluded from the Gondal poems of this
period. With its wars, exiled heroes and revolutionary students,
Gondal was coloured by the mood of the nineteenth century.

> *Their* feet shall never waken more
> The echoes in these galleries wide,
> Nor dare the snow on the mountain's brow,
> Nor skim the river's frozen flow,
> Nor wander down its side.
>
> They who have been our life – our soul –
> Through summer-youth, from childhood's spring –
> Who bound us in one vigorous whole
> To stand 'gainst Tyranny's control
> For ever triumphing –   (H104)

The evidence as to whether this was a people's or a monarchical
tyranny is contradictory. According to the voice of busy common
sense much of Emily Brontë's poetry represents an escape from an
intolerably narrow existence. One's response to the passions of
creatures whose world is partly shut-off from the modern reader
is inevitably limited; as it also is to the rather solipsistic response
to nature – a generalised ntaure – of the more personal poems. Yet
the wise and evidently hard-won detachment that enabled her to
realise the presence of nature, briefly,

> I watch this cloudy evening fall,
> After a day of rain:
> Blue mists, sweet mists of summer pall
> The horizon's mountain-chain.
>
> The damp stands in the long, green grass
> As thick as morning's tears . . .   (H113)
>
> I've seen the purple heather-bell
> Look out by many a storm-worn stone . . .   (H108)

as well as her own 'uncertainties, difficulties, doubts', is admirable. (But stones in her poetry are all too rarely individual and actual, like this one.) In her 1845 note the struggle to come to terms with her existence, and perhaps with her longing for transcendence, shows briefly: 'Having learnt to make the most of the present, and long for the future with [less?] fidgetiness . . .'[17]

'An imagination feeding quite wantonly on extremes of passion' is revealed in the Gondal poems, according to David Daiches. They are passionate, certainly, but not wanton or erotic. The cosmos of the Gondal love poems reveals not abandon, but a continual state of tension, an irresistible passion encounters an immovable morality. Passion can be indulged only at another's expense, and remorse and love are permanent and inescapable. Intensity of feeling must be paid for.

> Sweeter far than placid pleasure,
> Purer, higher, beyond measure,
> Yet alas the sooner turning
> Into hopeless, endless mourning.　　　(H112)

If the emotions felt in this world are so painful, to have to suffer retribution in the next is harsh indeed.

> Shall these long, agonising years
> Be punished by eternal tears?
>
> No! *that* I feel can never be;
> A God of *hate* could hardly bear
> To watch through all eternity
> His own creations dread despair!　　　(H133)

The tortuosity of some of Emily Brontë's poetry does, in an abstract way, embody the involvement of sin and retribution.

> Yet could I with past pleasures
> Past woe's oblivion buy,
> That by the death of my dearest treasures
> My deadliest pains might die . . .　　　(H120)

This is a world in which nothing is forgotten; an emotion, once experienced, remains dominant.

There let thy bleeding branch atone
For every torturing tear:
Shall my young sins, my sins alone,
Be everlasting here?

Who bade thee keep that cursed name
A pledge for memory?
As if Oblivion ever came
To breathe its bliss on me;

As if, through all the 'wildering maze
Of mad hours left behind,
I once forgot the early days
That thou wouldst call to mind.   (H142)

The now-emergent, later dominant, theme is the sense of the
incongruity of pain and evil with the splendour of nature. A state
of semi-permanent rebellion against the inadequacy of the Christian eschatology to provide any adequate answer to this situation
results. The abstraction of Christian bliss is no substitute for the
joy of earth. (Emily Brontë remained virtually silent in public on
the question of religion. Not in itself surprising, in this age it
was unusual.) Nevertheless the Christian cosmos continually
shapes the thought of the poems. These attitudes appear in a
group of poems significantly copied into her non-Gondal manuscript book in 1844, but dated early in 1841. Most important,
because most direct, is 'I see around me tombstones grey'. There
is too much woe on earth to forget in heaven: the angels are
happy, but see how inexperienced they are!

Sweet land of light! thy children fair
Know nought akin to our despair;
Nor have they felt, nor can they tell
What tenants haunt each mortal cell,
What gloomy guests we hold within –
Torments and madness, tears and sin!
Well, may they live in extasy
Their long eternity of joy;
At least we would not bring them down
With us to weep, with us to groan.

In this, in view of her background, rather daring poem, heaven is a cheat, seducing us from our rightful allegiance to earth.

> We would not leave our native home
> For *any* world beyond the Tomb.
> No – rather on thy kindly breast
> Let us be laid in lasting rest;
> Or waken but to share with thee
> A mutual immortality.   (H149)

The idea is, of course, repeated by Catherine Earnshaw in *Wuthering Heights* ('Heaven did not seem to be my home') and is an essential part of Emily Brontë's outlook. (This naturalism may be the legacy of a major poet to a less important one. The Preface to *Prometheus Unbound* states that 'one great poet is a masterpiece of nature which another not only ought to study, but must study', and the poem itself, that uneven but central statement of romanticism, contains the same characterisation of Earth as 'I see around me tombstones grey'.) A few days before the date on the poem, Emily wrote a kind of 'Ode to the West Wind', 'Aye, there it is! It wakes to-night' (H148).

> Yes, I could swear that glorious wind
> Has swept the world aside,
> Has dashed its memory from thy mind
> Like foam-bells from the tide –
>
> And thou art now a spirit pouring
> Thy presence into all –
> The essence of the Tempest's roaring
> And of the Tempest's fall –
>
> A universal influence
> From Thine own influence free;
> A principle of life, intense,
> Lost to mortality.

The response to Shelley, tempered with her own consciousness of the Christian world-picture, suggests that this most important influence dates from this time. It is, I think, manifest in later poems, and indirectly – but very revealingly – in *Wuthering Heights*.

Emily Brontë's poetry is thus an uncensored record of the growth of her mind. The side that her sister was allowed to see is apparent in the 1841 'birthday note', written in parallel with another by Anne. They evidently agreed to write them at four-yearly intervals and to open them together. The four papers were recovered by Shorter from the material kept by Mr Nicholls,[18] tightly folded like messages from secret agents. Emily's shows her putting a good face on the project to run a school of their own – part of the reason for their forthcoming studies on the Continent. The real reason, in Charlotte's case, was to a great extent the desire to escape to a fuller existence.

Emily's prose notes are evidence of a more compartmented mind than that of Emily Dickinson, for instance, whose poems and letters clearly come from the same region of their author's mind. The conflict between her ideas as revealed by, say, 'I see around me tombstones grey' and the orthodox family atmosphere may have had something to do with it, but reserve was also part of her nature. (She was, inconsistently, to drop it to some extent when writing for M. Heger.)

> A scheme is at present in agitation for setting us up in a school of our own; as yet nothing is determined, but I hope and trust it may go on and prosper, and answer our highest expectations. This day four years I wonder whether we shall still be dragging on in our present condition, or established to our heart's content. Time will show.
>
> I guess that at the time appointed for the opening of this paper, we, Charlotte, Anne and I, shall be all merrily seated in our own sitting room in some pleasant and flourishing seminary, having just gathered in for the midsummer ladyday. Our debts will be paid off, and we shall have cash in hand to a considerable amount. Papa aunt and Branwell will either have been or be coming to visit us. It will be a fine warm summer evening, very different from this bleak look-out, and Anne and I will perchance slip out into the garden for a few minutes to peruse our papers.[19]

'Dragging on in our present condition' – the Tennysonian accents of lassitude are less predictable in Emily than in her sisters, who

were both enduring situations away from home. In her parallel
note Anne Brontë recorded: 'This is Emily's birthday. She has
now completed her 23rd year, and is, I believe, at home.' (Her
being at home seems not to have been such an accepted state of
affairs.) Anne's reference to Law Hill solves no problems. 'Emily
has been a teacher at Miss Patchet's [*sic*] school, and left it.'

Whether they took over Miss Wooler's school, which had
been offered, or ran their own at the parsonage, they would
need languages. Their friends the Taylors were already at a
Brussels finishing school, and the city was noted for a low cost of
living and good teachers. To Charlotte, the guiding spirit,
Brussels meant much more than diplomas in languages – it meant
freedom and culture.

It seems that Emily would have preferred that they take over
the Wooler school. No prospect, evidently, could have been less
welcome than a Catholic school in the Low Countries. She had,
as might be expected, to be persuaded to accompany her sister,
rather than Anne, who, as governess, deserved the education more,
and whose claims Emily advocated.[20] The reasons for Charlotte's
insistence that the prior claim was Emily's and her readiness to
take her to continental exile after the Roe Head 'failure' and her
anxiety about her at Law Hill can only be conjectural. It may not
be indulging in undue partisanship to suggest that she needed
Emily's mature companionship and good sense. But when sum-
marising this period in the Preface already discussed, Charlotte
described her sister undergoing another crisis. 'Once more she
seemed sinking, but this time she rallied through the mere force
of resolution: with inward remorse and shame she looked back on
her former failure, and resolved to conquer in this second ordeal.'[21]
Perhaps, but there is nothing about this in Charlotte's letters at
the time. The pattern of contradictions in the evidence about
Emily Brontë in Brussels seems partly a result of afterthoughts by
various witnesses. Another contradiction is Mary Taylor's comment to Mrs Gaskell (reported in *The Life of Charlotte Brontë*), that
in London, where they stayed on their way to Brussels in February
1842, the reserved Emily seemed well informed, like her sister,
and 'certainly never took her opinion, but always had one to offer'.

'Little gained, at vast expense', she wrote in a poem shortly before leaving the pensionnat. At this time she was not much concerned with worldly or cultural accomplishments. Like Novalis, with whom she has been compared, she created for herself in the visible world an invisible one. Her seriousness, to judge from the poems already mentioned, had long since eliminated any merely facile Byronism. Her reflective and fundamentally religious cast of mind was tinged with world-weariness and nihilism, contending with traditional faith.

> Look on the grave where thou must sleep,
> Thy last and strongest foe;
> 'Twill be endurance not to weep
> If that repose be woe.   (H155)

Almost from the first, Emily Brontë's preoccupation with death is absolutely fundamental to her artistic character. It may have originated in Evangelicalism, but its outcome was very un-Evangelical. Her sense of life, and of the importance of intense feeling, 'Sweeter far than placid pleasure', was also strong. She went to Brussels at a time when romanticism was in flood in the French-speaking countries, when de Nerval, on the banks of the Rhine, could exclaim, 'le pays d'Hoffmann!' Unfortunately her conversations with her teachers must remain largely imaginary, apart from the few facts reported by Mrs Gaskell. Yet a singular aspect of her work, or one that would be more singular in another writer, is the exclusion of any direct trace of the Brussels months.

The background is familiar (and has recently been re-created in great detail by Miss W. Gérin[22]). Much, nevertheless, remains unclear concerning the characters of the Hegers, those respected Brussels figures, and their exact relations with the two Brontës.

It was an ironic encounter between a teacher with a more than average interest in writing and the sisters who had been writing for most of their lives. Heger's instruction combined the enlightened and the dryly pedantic. He taught French direct and seems to have known little English. Emily's struggle to overcome her weakness in languages is evident, though according to Mrs Gaskell they could both read it fluently. (Emily wrote fewer poems than at any comparable period of her life during these months.)

> Emily and he don't draw well together at all. When he is very ferocious with me I cry; that sets all things straight. Emily works like a horse, and she has had great difficulties to contend with, far greater than I have had.[23]

His relationship with female pupils was very personal, perhaps mildly flirtatious,[24] and *a priori* Emily Brontë must have refused any relationship of the kind that affected her sister so deeply. She openly disagreed with his academic instruction in writing – mainly by copying stylistic gems. But there was another side to his teaching: his contemporaries left many tributes to his brilliance and sympathy, his talent for arousing his pupils' interest. It was no commonplace mind that appealed to Charlotte so strongly.[25] He was interested in the strategy of creative work, telling students 'not to fight with a difficult sentence, but to take it for a walk with one, or sleep with it present in one's mind'.[26] In addition to the sympathy of the artist *manqué*, M. Heger manifested a devout Catholicism[27] in a school in which the basis of the curriculum was religion.[28] It is tempting to read something of his clash with Emily in the passage in *Villette* where Paul Emanuel, the French instructor, exclaims against English women, 'their slovenly dress, their pedantic education, their impious scepticism, their insufferable pride'.[29] (Emily was careless about her dress, according to their co-pupils in Brussels the Wheelwright sisters.[30])

Her surviving devoirs reveal her outlook on man as, approximately, a social, political and religious being; they show Emily Brontë the 'Philosopher' and the woman. The classroom forced her ideas into the open. (Emily's fine, regular spiky longhand suggests a temperament of great precision: the essays are set out like ledger entries.) Trenchant and well shaped, 'Le Chat' has a characteristically sardonic quality; it is the first statement in prose of her romantic misanthropy, pessimism, and dislike of convention. Hervey's *Meditations* and Wesley's *Compendium of Natural Philosophy*,[31] the seventeenth-century 'character' and the French *physiologie* are possible models.

le chat, encore qu'il diffère en quelque points physiques, est extrêment semblable à nous en disposition.

Il peut etre des gens, en vérité, qui diraient que cette ressemblance ne lui approche qu'aux hommes les plus méchants; qu'elle est bornée a son exces de hypocrisie, de cruaute et d'ingratitude, vices détestables dans notre race et également odieux en celle des chats . . . je reponds, que si l'hypocrisie, le cruaute et l'ingratitude sont exclusivement la propriété des méchants, cette classe renferme tout le monde. . . .

(the cat, although he differs in some physical traits, is extremely like us in disposition.

In truth, there may be people who would say that the resemblance is close only in the meanest human beings, that it is limited to their excessive hypocrisy, cruelty and ingratitude – detestable vices in our species and equally odious in the cat's . . . I answer that if hypocrisy, cruelty and ingratitude are the characteristics exclusively of mean people, this class includes everyone . . .)

notre education [she wrote, tactlessly] développe une de ces qualites en grande perfection, les autres fleurissent sans soin, et loin de les condamner nous regardons tous les trois avec beaucoup de complaisance.

(our education develops one of these qualities in great perfection, the others thrive without cultivation, and we, far from condemning them, look upon all three with great complacency.)

(Translations of Emily Brontë's French, which was written after three months' formal instruction, tend to flatter it. M. Bellour, who is preparing a French edition of the Brontës' works, has called it 'plus qu'hésitant'.)

After selecting these Victorian domestic vices of hypocrisy and cruelty she concentrates on the latter. A sensitive lady 'who has murdered half a dozen lap-dogs in pure affection' would accuse the cat of cruelty, but her husband hunts bagged foxes, and though she dare not be in at the death herself, she encourages cruelty in her children.

J'ai vous vue embrasser avec transport votre enfant quand il [?]
vous montrer un beau papillon écrasé entre ses cruels petits
doigts; at à ce moment, j'ai voulu bien avoir un chat avec la
queue d'un rat demi englouti, pendant de sa bouche, à pre-
senter comme l'image, la vraie copie de votre ange; vous ne
pourriez refuser de le baiser, et s'il vous égratignait tous deux
en revanche, tant mieux, les petits garcons sont assez liables à
reconnaître ainsi les caresses de leur amis, et la ressemblance
serait plus parfaite.[32]

(I have seen you enthusiastically hug your child when he [ran?]
to show you a beautiful butterfly crushed between his cruel little
fingers; then I would very much like to have had a cat with the
tail of a half-swallowed rat hanging from his mouth to show
you, as the exact image of your little angel; you could not help
but kiss him, and if he scratched you both in revenge, so much
the better, little boys are quite likely thus to greet the caresses of
their friends, and the resemblance would be so much the better.)

It suggests a savage parody of John Earle's sentimental 'character'
of the child. She concludes:

The ingratitude of cats is another word for penetration. They
know how to value our favours, because they know the motives
behind them. And if these are sometimes good, they undoubtedly remember that they owe all their good and bad
qualities to the great ancestor of the human race, for certainly
the cat was not bad in Paradise.

The actual workings of a poetic imagination may contradict its
direct statement of its ideas, but these devoirs throw light on the
nature of *Wuthering Heights*. They show that, as with Breughel or
Bosch, Emily's images of cruelty are placed in a religious or
cosmological frame; they arise in speculation about the nature
of man and reality.

'Whenever the Brontës could be national, they were so', wrote
Mrs Gaskell.[33] Emily's 'Portrait du roi Harold avant la bataille'
was written after Heger had read them Hugo's portrait of Mira-
beau, and analysed its design and (one can hear him) 'ce qu'on
pourrait appeler la charpente'.[34] Harold was much admired in the

early nineteenth century. His portrait here lacks the bite of 'The Cat'. It shows a stereotyped hero freed from the falsities of the court to face the ultimate reality of death.

> He has an inner conviction that no mortal power can defeat him. Only the hand of death can gain the victory over his arms, and Harold is ready to cede to him, because to the hero the touch of that hand is like the stroke that liberates the slave.[35]

Heger's pencilled criticism of the aptness of the final simile can still be deciphered. It is a clue to their failure to 'draw well together'.

'Le Papillon' was written later in the summer of 1842. Whereas 'Le Chat' is a recognisable if 'sick' and inverted piece from the bestiary, in 'Le Papillon' the treatment is quite different. It opens on a deeply personal note. The author is meditating on the cruelty of nature and is in one of those moods 'lorsque le monde de l'imagination souffre un hiver', the metaphor is terse and beautiful as if from the pen of a Benjamin Constant. The essay makes an unsuccessful attempt to reconcile a *mondo cane* with Christian belief. (To Emily the human species enjoyed no special category of suffering.)

> l'univers me paraissait une vaste machine construit seulement pour produire le mal: je doutais presque de la bonté de Dieu, dans ce qu'il n'anéantit pas l'homme sur le jour du premier peche. 'Le monde aussi dû étre detruit', je dis 'écrasé comme j'écrase ce reptile qui n'a fait rien pendant sa vie que de rendre tout ce qu'il touche aussi dégoùtant que lui meme.'[36]

> (the universe seemed to me a vast machine made solely to produce evil: I doubted even the goodness of God for not destroying man on the day of his first sin. 'The world too, should be destroyed', I said, 'wiped out as I wipe out this reptile that has done nothing in its life but to make everything it touches as disgusting as itself.')

Her rose, destroyed by the caterpillar, is sick, and it is difficult to see how the sudden appearance of the butterfly, a moment of beauty that rebukes the thinker as a symbol of the world to come – 'an inner voice reminded me that the creature should not judge his creator' – is an adequate answer to the universe of cruelty already evoked, in which pain and beauty exist side by side. The forceful *Weltschmerz* of the opening is telling enough to make one wonder whether the pious coda was written for M. Heger, and the 'cours d'instruction basé sur la religion' of the pensionnat. But the essay contains two poles of her reflection, which veers between heterodox extremes and near-orthodoxy. Its thought, in 'the saint leaves enough misery here below to sadden him even before the throne of God', is identical to that of 'I see around me tombstones grey', but the conclusion is different. Here, too, the comparison with *Wuthering Heights* is interesting. The essay provides a statement of the element of nineteenth-century rationalism implicit in the novel, and its imagery recurs in the famous closing paragraph ('watched the moths fluttering among the heath and hare-bells') in a context of which the meaning is more equivocal and more satisfying.

In July 1842 Charlotte was hoping that they would be able to stay on in Brussels after the autumn: 'Mme Heger has made a proposal for both me and Emily to stay another half-year – offering to dismiss her English master and take me as teacher – also to employ Emily some part of each day as in [sic] teaching music . . .'[37] The Hegers were 'beginning to recognise the valuable parts of her nature under her singularities'. But, as with a recent moral extremist such as Simone Weil, reactions varied. 'I simply disliked her from the first', wrote one of their co-pupils, Laetitia Wheelwright.

> Her tallish, ungainly, ill-dressed figure contrasting so strongly with Charlotte's trim, neat person, although their dresses were alike, always answering our jokes with: 'I wish to be as God made me.' She taught my three youngest sisters music for four months, to my annoyance, as she would only take them in play hours, naturally causing many tears to small children, the eldest ten, the youngest seven. Fortunately she was summoned home in November, and did not return to Brussels. Charlotte was so devotedly attached to her, and thought so highly of her talents.[38]

Another English family found her throughout 'as impenetrable to friendly advances as at the beginning', but for Mlle Bassompierre, a Belgian pupil, 'Mlle Emilie was much less brilliant, but much more sympathetic than her sister. She was working hard at drawing, and had become very skilled. She gave me an attractive signed landscape, which I have carefully kept . . .'[39]

There has been so much speculation about her knowledge of German that Charlotte's reference to her rapid progress is interesting, as the only evidence. (The vignette of Diana Rivers, in *Jane Eyre* reading German is suggestive, but inconclusive.) The extent of her knowledge of German literature in the original is unknown. The indications in *Wuthering Heights*, considered below, point to possible familiarity with translations. The compounds in her poems, 'overfly', 'undergloom', 'seablue', 'seadeep' are suggestive, but probably Tennysonian, if not entirely her own.

At moments she evidently sought 'another clime, another sky' during the Low Countries' summer. Her poetic landscape had never been more northern than in 'Written in Aspin Castle' (H154), dated 20 August 1842 and 6 February 1843 and evidently finished after her return.

> How do I love to hear the flow
> Of Aspin's water murmuring low;
> And hours long listen to the breeze
> That sighs in Rockden's waving trees.
>
> To-night, there is no wind to wake
> One ripple on the lonely lake;
> To-night, the clouds subdued and grey
> Starlight and moonlight shut away.

Her 'Palace of Death' essay, begun in the new school half in October, is not necessarily connected with a series of deaths in the Brontës' limited circle during the last months of 1842. (The curate William Weightman died of cholera at Haworth in September, and their fellow-pupil in Brussels, Martha Taylor, also in October, while Miss Branwell's death was imminent.) The subject was evidently set for them, since Charlotte produced a very similar essay. The immediate example or source is not known,

but it has been shown to be the type of *fable* so dear to the classi-
cising French mind. Emily's 'Palais de la Mort' is a *danse
macabre*, with some touches worthy of Bunyan; it shows how well
she could bring the allegorical form to life. Intemperance, the
mysterious stranger before whom all the contestants for the office
of Death's Prime Minister must give way, 'avait une figure qui
paraissait rayonner de joie et de santé', and even Death is uneasy
at her approach. But she is there simply to herald the approach of
Civilisation, 'before whom this whole assembly will be forced to
yield'. The presence of Civilisation in such company is com-
promising and it would be interesting to know whether Emily
departed from her source in order to be ironical at the expense of
Victorian meliorism. Intemperance and civilisation are similarly
associated with death in one of Florian's *Fables* published in 1792.[40]

M. Heger's appreciation of the devoirs is apparent in his
tribute to Emily, as reported by Mrs Gaskell.

He seems to have rated Emily's genius as something even higher
than Charlotte's; and her estimation of their relative powers
was the same. Emily had a head for logic and a capability of
argument, unusual in a man and rare indeed in a woman,
according to M. Heger. Impairing the force of this gift was a
stubborn tenacity of will which rendered her obtuse to all
reasoning where her own wishes, or her own sense of right was
concerned. 'She should have been a man – a great navigator,'
said M. Heger, in speaking of her. 'Her powerful reason would
have deduced new spheres of discovery from the knowledge of
the old; and her strong imperious will would never have been
daunted by opposition or difficulty; never have given way but
with life.' And yet, moreover, her faculty of imagination was
such that, if she had written a history, her view of scenes and
characters would have been so vivid and so powerfully expressed
and supported by such a show of argument, that it would have
dominated over the reader, whatever might have been his
cooler perceptions of its truth. But she appeared egotistical and
exacting compared with Charlotte, who was always unselfish
[this is M. Heger's testimony]; and in the anxiety of the elder
to make her younger sister contented, she allowed her to exercise a kind of unconscious tyranny over her.[41]

The sombre autobiographical poem 'The evening passes fast away' (H155), the last dated in Brussels (though it was finished in Haworth according to its second date), is unillumined even by the delight in nature she was to recover sometimes at home. In part it is a recapitulation of the themes of the devoirs, a dialogue between world-weariness, a flickering sense of life, and some form of religious promise.

> The evening passes fast away,
> 'Tis almost time to rest;
> What thoughts has left the vanished day?
> What feelings in thy breast?
>
> 'The vanished day? It leaves a sense
> Of labour hardly done;
> Of little gained with vast expense –
> A sense of grief alone!
>
> 'Time stands before the door of Death,
> Upbraiding bitterly;
> And Conscience, with exhaustless breath,
> Pours black reproach on me:
>
> 'And though I think that Conscience lies,
> And Time should Fate condemn;
> Still, weak Repentance clouds my eyes,
> And makes me yield to them!'

It is a partial denial of the repentance of the 'Butterfly' essay, and though the poem closes piously, it does so without the force of these first stanzas. (Her poetic strength, in her 'late' poems, is largely the ability to do without orthodox reassurance. As belief narrows, the artistic integrity of the poems increases.)

Mary Taylor's letters to Ellen Nussey during and after this period show that any alleviation of Emily's usual *terribiltà* was a matter of comment. She recorded her impressions of her taciturnity during an evening following a visit to her sister Martha's grave near Brussels (an occasion reproduced in *Shirley*) and found Miss Nussey's report – that she had become more accessible – difficult to square with them.[42] M. Heger's letter to Mr Brontë, when their aunt's death caused their sudden return, could be taken as confirming Miss Nussey: 'Mlle Emily was learning the piano, and having lessons from the best teacher in Belgium; already she had her own pupils; hence she was losing both the rest of her ignorance and, of what was worse, her shyness.'[43]

But this coolness in 1842, compared with the warmth reported by Mrs Gaskell above, indicates that by then a legend was in being, after the publication of *Wuthering Heights* and its author's death.

IV

THE remarkable development in Emily Brontë's poetry during those last years of family stress and achievement can be linked with outward events only to a problematic extent. Miss Branwell's death provided the sisters with some means of their own, and at this time Emily began to take a larger share in their affairs. With both sisters away from home, she invested some of the legacy in the railways. She read 'every paragraph in the news papers relating to rail roads'[1] (there were frequent announcements of new promotions). Charlotte's later comment that her powers were 'unadapted to the practical business of life'[2] may have been influenced by their disagreements about these investments. In fact, in the practical sense, she was not so remote from the modern joint-stock world so rapidly developing during her lifetime as her sister's memoirs suggest.

In her lonely, and increasingly awkward, position of unrequited attachment to the husband of her employer in Brussels, Charlotte confided in her sister to some extent. Their letters (one of Emily's from this time has survived) reveal their understanding of each other's character. 'I went in alone', Charlotte wrote of the confessional incident she used in *Villette*, adding, '(which procedure you will say is not much like me).'[3] Emily's attitude to the use of language is apparent in the earliest of her few surviving letters (addressed to Miss Nussey).

Charlotte has never mentioned a word about coming home, if you would go over for half a year perhaps you might be able to bring her back with you, otherwise she may vegetate there till the age of Methuselah for mere lack of courage to face the voyage . . . the holydays will be here in a week or two, and then, if she [i.e. Anne] be willing, I will get her to write you a proper letter – a feat I have never performed.[4]

'The Major', her nickname among their immediate circle, is here evident. During the subsequent months the idea of keeping their own school, either elsewhere or at home, proved impossible; the former because their father's sight was failing, and the latter because no pupils were available. Emily made her views, and perhaps those of them all, plain in her 1845 note: 'we had prospectuses printed, despatched letters to all our acquaintances imparting our plans, and did our little all, but it was found no go. Now I don't desire a school at all, and none of us have any great longing for it.'⁵ Though he was still employed with the same family as Anne, their brother's dissipation and instability made the school project doubtful in any case.

Both of Emily's transcript notebooks are headed 'Transcribed February 1844'. These, the 'Gondal Poems', and the 'Honresfeld' manuscript contain the greater proportion of her poetry and show that the much-argued distinction between poetry relating to fictional situations and autobiographical or 'personal' poetry is one she tried to maintain. Both are written in her small, compressed script. The Gondal book was used for composing a new poem at the end of her life, and terminates in alterations and blots.

The notebooks give a blurred glimpse of her at work. Despite the headings 'Transcribed February', the work, like most such copying, took much longer. For instance, the long Gondal poem with a curiously logistical heading 'A.G.A., The Death Of', was not fully written (according to the dates on it) until May 1844. Several much earlier poems come after it in the Gondal book, indicating that transcription continued until May at least. One can tell approximately when transcription of earlier poems was complete, since the poems begin to be copied-in in chronological order. The 'personal' poems were transcribed by about March 1844 and the Gondal poems in May. Earlier poems are not arranged chronologically, but according to Gondal characters in the one case and to some extent by tone and mood in the other. There was a certain amount of revision. Alterations made in her script writing on earlier manuscripts, such as the fragment of a notebook in longhand⁶ which may have been an earlier Gondal book, were almost certainly made at this time. Transcription is apt to result in revision, not only of the work, but also of the writer's view of himself. It may be only coincidence that most of her finest poems were written soon after this conspectus.

In the meditative and increasingly 'personal' poems of mid and late 1844, the inner debate affirms her solitary commitment to the imagination with increased conviction, though not without signs of stress – the 'savage heart'. As in the close of 'My Comforter' (H168).

> And yet a little longer speak,
> Calm this resentful mood,
> And while the savage heart grows meek,
> For other token do not seek,
> But let the tear upon my cheek
> Evince my gratitude.

The 'ever present, phantom thing' (H176) seems to be the imagination seen in religious terms. Creativity offers some of the comforts of religion, but it is also as relentless as God. For it the world is renounced. It is also a refuge. In 'My Comforter' there is emphasis on the involuntary aspect.

> Thou hast but roused a latent thought,
> A cloud-closed beam of sunshine brought
> To gleam in open view.

There are (perhaps) suggestions of her troubled family.

> Was I not vexed, in these gloomy ways
> To walk unlit so long?
> Around me, wretches uttering praise,
> Or howling o'er their hopeless days,
> And each with Frenzy's tongue.
>
> A Brotherhood of misery,
> With smiles as sad as sighs . . .

One notes that the accents of Puritan conversion are appropriate to this salvation by another kind of inner light. This subjective relationship gives rise to the suggestions of mysticism in these poems, but later the ecstatic experience is more powerful and less easily defined. 'I trust not to thy phantom bliss,' she writes, in a poem headed 'To Imagination' (H174). But the imagination is seen in its true character: it is fitful – 'a little longer speak' – it is 'My slave, my comrade, and my King!' (H176). The diction and manner of this self-scrutiny owe something to George Herbert, but the choices, as mentioned, are different.

> No, radiant angel, speak and say
> Why I did cast the world away;
>
> Why I have persevered to shun
> The common paths that others run;
> And on a strange road journeyed on
> Heedless alike of Wealth and Power –
> Of Glory's wreath and Pleasure's flower.
>
> These once indeed seemed Beings divine,
> And they perchance heard vows of mine
> And saw my offerings on their shrine –
> But, careless gifts are seldom prized,
> And mine were worthily despised . . .   (H176)

The method is often that of paradox; the statements have an out-of-context meaning contradictory to their meaning in the poem.

> And yet, a king – though prudence well
> Have taught thy subject to rebel.

Here prudence, the world's concerns, constitutes a rebellion against the sovereign imagination. Just as a line like

> Thy love I will not, will not share   (H157)

is part of a statement of renunciation (sharing – 'dividing with' or 'partaking of'). Spiritual logic is paradoxical. The language of *Wuthering Heights* often derives its energy from a similar process. But there is, it seems to me, an element of artistic pharisaism about these poems, as if Emily Brontë is more concerned over generalised ideas of the world's ills than those within her immediate sphere. It makes them, perhaps undeservedly, difficult to

live with, more so, certainly than Herbert's. The same can be said
of 'How beautiful the Earth is still' (H188) of June 1845, which
need not be interpreted as a comment on the unhappy attach-
ments of her sister and brother (though such interpretation is
tempting).

> When those who were thy own compeers,
> Equal in fortunes and in years,
> Have seen their morning melt in tears,
> To dull, unlovely day:
> Blest, had they died unproved and young
> Before their hearts were wildly wrung,
> Poor slaves, subdued by passions strong,
> A weak and helpless prey!

Such sentiments are inappropriate to the opening theme of the
poem; the god of the imagination has, one feels, become the
Evangelical god of cant.

Subsequent, and finer, poems were to be written during the last
half of 1845 and early 1846 in a family atmosphere of impending
or actual crisis. Their father's sight was seriously threatened. In
July 1845, just before Emily's twenty-seventh birthday, Charlotte, though reluctant to leave him, was hoping to visit Ellen
Nussey when Anne and her brother were back from their employ-
ment for the holiday. 'I do so long to be with you', she wrote,
'and feel nervously afraid of being prevented.'[7] But first her sisters
were able to make an excursion recorded in Emily's birthday
note:

> leaving home on the 30th of June, Monday, sleeping at York,
> returning to Keighley Tuesday evening . . . sleeping there and
> walking home Wednesday morning . . . during our excursion we
> were Ronald Macalgin, Henry Angora, Juliet Angusteena,
> escaping from the palaces of instruction to join the royal-
> ists . . .[8]

Childhood's enduring hold on adult Victorian women has seldom
been more strikingly revealed, or the Brontës' ability to move from
unpleasant reality to fantasy. A week later she was writing Miss
Nussey, in the second of her surviving letters, to reassure her
sister: 'let her make the most of the next seven days to return

stout and hearty . . . tell her all are well at home'.[9] Charlotte's return to find that events had accelerated her brother's final disintegration has often been described. Many have endorsed her subsequent severity towards him. There is a tradition that Emily in reality was less detached and more sympathetic than the poems quoted suggest. Certainly this moral trial, to which they reacted differently, seems to be reflected in these and later poems. (One notes her creation of the unrewarded sympathy of the young Catherine, in *Wuthering Heights*, for an abject Linton.)

'The Philosopher', 'Stars', 'Remembrance', 'The Prisoner' and 'No coward soul is mine' were all written between February 1845 and January 1846. These are the poems by which Emily Brontë is known. She had written fine lyrics and other poems of interest in the total context of her work, but this note of sustained power is new. The often merely conventional Victorian versifier becomes a poet of powerfully expressed doubt and inner conflict, but one not always easily interpreted.

The anthologists' omission of 'The Philosopher' is curious. Dated 3 February 1845, it was thus titled for the 1846 *Poems*, but there is no title in the only manuscript version. This poem made an immediate impression on Emily Brontë's contemporaries when published in the 1846 volume. We can perhaps go further than the Scottish essayist Peter Bayne, who wrote:

> Whether it is in the mere dramatic sympathy of the artist that Emily Brontë puts words into the mouth of the Philosopher, or whether the words are her own, and reveal a secret that might throw some light on her stern, reserved and ungenial existence, and on the mood of mind in which *Wuthering Heights* was composed – I shall not undertake to decide.[10]

The poem (to give a rather pedestrian reading) consists of the Philosopher's cry for an end to inner conflict, after an introductory stanza.

> 'O for the time when I shall sleep
> Without identity,
> And never care how rain may steep
> Or snow may cover me!

'No promised Heaven, these wild Desires
Could all or half fulfil;
No threathened [*sic*] Hell, with quenchless fires,
Subdue this quenchless will!'

– So said I, and still say the same;
– Still to my Death will say –
Three Gods within this little frame
Are warring night and day.

Heaven could not hold them all, and yet
They all are held in me
And must be mine till I forget
My present entity.   (H181)

(The first two stanzas quoted are underlined in the manuscript,
they are the 'sad refrain' of the opening stanza.) To this statement
the Seer replies with a vision of harmony.

'I saw a Spirit standing, Man,
Where thou dost stand – an hour ago;
And round his feet, three rivers ran
Of equal depth and equal flow –

'A Golden stream, and one like blood,
And one like Sapphire, seemed to be,
But where they joined their triple flood
It tumbled in an inky sea.

'The Spirit bent his dazzling gaze
Down on that Ocean's gloomy night,
Then – kindling all with sudden blaze,
The glad deep sparkled wide and bright –
White as the sun; far, far more fair
Than the divided sources were!'

Unable to confirm it in his own experience, the Philosopher concludes with a recapitulation of the plea for oblivion.

– And even for that Spirit, Seer,
I've watched and sought my lifetime long;
Sought Him in Heaven, Hell, Earth and Air,
An endless search – and always wrong!

Had I but seen his glorious eye
Once light the clouds that 'wilder me,
I ne'er had raised this coward cry
To cease to think and cease to be –

I ne'er had called oblivion blest,
Nor stretching eager hands to Death
Implored to change for lifeless rest
This sentient soul, this living breath.

O let me die, that power and will
Their cruel strife may close,
And vanquished Good, victorious Ill
Be lost in one repose.

The machinery, the dialogue between the Philosopher (Emily
Brontë in the totality of her mental life) and the Seer, the vehicle
for the vision of the ideal, and of inner harmony, the goal of her
search for God, seems inessential. Nevertheless there is a force of
feeling, a directness and economy of statement that transcends this
troublesome outer structure. Identity is clearly implied between
the 'Three Gods within this little frame' of the Philosopher's
statement and the three rivers of the vision. The warring gods are
also connected with 'these wild desires' and with the strife of
power and will of the final stanza.

'The Philosopher' was written by someone whose ideas were
perhaps not clear even to herself, and who was reluctant to disclose
them in any event; it seems to contain something unrealised. But
it is also a poem that goes to the heart of her experience.

The imagery is, however, Biblical, as well as somewhat Shelley-
an. It may derive from Revelation, itself a darkly personal as
well as a religious and political document. The relevant texts are
8 : 8 and 15 : 2.

. . . and the third part of the sea became blood.
And I saw as it were a sea of glass mingled with fire : and them
that had gotten the victory over the beast, and over his image,
and over his mark, and over the number of his name, stand on
the sea of glass, having the harps of God.

Three anonymous warring gods, three symbolic rivers whose

confluence is the 'inky sea' (of death?), the associations with guilt of the river of blood suggested by the context in Revelation are supported by the conflict of good and ill of the final stanza. Likewise, the vision of wholeness is presented in the imagery of the 'water of life, clear as crystal, proceeding out of the throne of God' of the same Biblical text. The vision, with its mandala-like image of a spiritual form combined with the confluence of the rivers, is strikingly suggestive (in Jungian terms) of the dreams associated with the process of individuation. Such dreams, Jung reported, are characteristic of patients unable to find god outside themselves. 'There is no deity in the modern mandala.' But the trinitarian vision is evidently recurrent in the religious consciousness.

Though the vision seems to derive from religious sources, it follows a specific rejection of an orthodox heaven, which is inadequate to contain the warring gods of the personality. (Similarly, in 'I see around me tombstones grey', the children of heaven have no inkling of the 'gloomy guests we hold within'.) 'The Philosopher' is another instance of the extreme subjectivism of the more considerable of the Brontës' works. It expresses a familiar dilemma. High romanticism, 'these wild desires' of the kind indulged to their unsatisfactory limit by Shelley, in *Epipsychidion*, is here forbidden by the moral law. God, the ultimate reality that might justify such a denial, has absconded ('an endless search, and always wrong'). Death is the only escape-route. The implied connection between the three conflicting gods, the rivers and the strife of good and ill indicates that the transcendent must take account of the specifically human. Emily Brontë's awareness of the need for personal fulfilment complicates the search for revelation. In the last stanza 'power' is perhaps a characteristically Victorian euphemism for the Id, the instinctual life. Thus 'The Philosopher' is about the uses of the psyche, the source of creativity, and of a sense of the transcendent. Emily Brontë's cryptically expressed insight is remarkable and courageous.

Obviously Peter Bayne was on the right track in the nineteenth century when he suggested a special connection between this poem and *Wuthering Heights*. If not evident already, the connection will

become so on closer consideration of the novel. 'The Philosopher'
is an embryo or codified statement of what the book is about. One
could say that the achievement of the vision, the finding of the
unifying spirit, can only be in the achieved form of the novel.
But there are difficulties in the way of such a neat view.

'The Philosopher' is a more interesting, if less straightforward,
poem than 'Remembrance' (3 March 1845 – H182), one poem
by Emily Brontë that everybody knows, and about which little
need be said. Her technically most assured work (stemming from
the earliest influences) consists of such lyrics in the Byronic mode,
one nearer to actual song than to the symbolic lyric of Blake.
But 'some strength, corresponding to "these brown hills" which
do not themselves melt, underlies the poem'.[11] 'Stars' (14 April
1845 – H184) seems to me one of her finest poems. It is an
all-too-rare realisation of a *particular* experience.

> Why did the morning rise to break
> So great, so pure a spell,
> And scorch with fire the tranquil cheek
> Where your cool radiance fell?
>
> Blood-red he rose, and arrow-straight
> His fierce beams struck my brow:
> The soul of Nature sprang elate,
> But mine sank sad and low!
>
> My lids closed down – yet through their veil
> I saw him blazing still;
> And bathe in gold the misty dale,
> And flash upon the hill.
>
> I turned me to the pillow then
> To call back Night, and see
> Your worlds of solemn light, again
> Throb with my heart and me!
>
> It would not do – the pillow glowed
> And glowed both roof and floor,
> And birds sang loudly in the wood,
> And fresh winds shook the door.

> The curtains waved, the wakened flies
> Were murmuring round my room,
> Imprisoned there, till I should rise
> And give them leave to roam.

The poem is strong enough to absorb minor flaws. The petrel of a preceding stanza is as irrelevant as Keats's 'deceiving elf' in the 'Nightingale' ode.

> I was at peace, and drank your beams
> As they were life to me
> And revelled in my changeful dreams
> Like petrel on the sea.

Despite the evocation of the primitive roots of mood,

> Blood-red he rose, and arrow-straight
> His fierce beams struck my brow:
> The soul of Nature sprang elate . . .

(and such transitions affect our inner lives to a greater extent than we admit), part of the effect of the poem derives from the fact that mood is often less unrelated to reality than it seems. 'Stars' is about the incompatibility of the inner world of fancy and the outer one of harsh fact. For the romantic the day can be dreadful because it means business, and one wonders whether this poem, in which the red ball of the newly risen sun is suffused with blood, and the dewdrops are tears, reveals consciousness of the human cost exacted by the society of the 1840s. It was written in the month in which she had been reading 'every paragraph in the news papers related to rail roads'. Some commentators have suggested that this is a Gondal poem, but if it is 'by' a fictional character Emily Brontë evidently considered it personal enough to be excluded from the manuscript book of Gondal poems. Miss Visick[12] has shown, though, that this personal statement of the opposition between the night and the dangerous vitality of the sun is anticipated by various versions of the undated Gondal poem 'To A.G.A.' ('Thou standest in the greenwood now' – H110) and that their imagery appears again in the opposition between Heathcliff and Edgar in *Wuthering Heights*. It seems possible, if my reading above is correct, that Emily Brontë was drawing conclusions (long before Hannah Arendt) from her own psyche, about Victorian *laisser faire* and the 'condition of England'. There is a further association between Heathcliff–Satan and the sun if, as I suspect, the end of the poem echoes Marlowe's *Doctor Faustus*.

> O Stars, and Dreams and Gentle Night;
> O Night and Stars return!
> And hide me from the hostile light
> That does not warm, but burn –

'The stars move still, time runs, the clock will strike.'[13] Satan, too, is Lucifer.

The long Gondal poem 'Julian M. and A. G. Rochelle', dated the following autumn, contains the well-known lines published in the 1846 volume as 'The Prisoner – A Fragment'. In view of the incongruity of this deeply felt statement with the Gothic scenery of dungeon and jailor against which it occurs, the Gondal situation seems largely irrelevant. Nevertheless these were the circumstances of its creation; they were a means of distancing the more personal core of the poem. ('Julian' seems to be the aspiring but anonymous republican of a later poem, ' Why ask to know the date – the clime?')

The opening of the poem, of which the following lines are a sample, recalls that source-book of Victorian medievalism, Keats's *The Eve of St Agnes*.

> Silent is the House – all are laid asleep;
> One, alone, looks out o'er the snow wreaths deep;
> Watching every cloud, dreading every breeze
> That whirls the 'wildering drifts and bends the groaning
>   trees.
>
> Cheerful is the hearth, soft the matted floor;
> Not one shivering gust creeps through pane or door;
> The little lamp burns straight, its rays shoot strong and far;
> I trim it well to be the Wanderer's guiding-star.

Frown, my haughty sire; chide, my angry dame;
Set your slaves to spy, threaten me with shame:
But neither sire nor dame, nor prying serf shall know
What angel nightly tracks that waste of winter snow. (H190)

The comparison of these much-quoted lines with Keats's is not
favourable to Emily Brontë. (Her sister added eight lines of her
own to the poem as printed in 1850, but her interpolation is less
unfortunate here than elsewhere.) Instead of Keats's luxurious
eroticism one has a certain sadistic feeling in Julian's visit to the
chained Rochelle.

Then, God forgive my youth, forgive my careless tongue!
I scoffed, as the chill chains on the damp flagstones rung;
'Confined in triple walls, art thou so much to fear,
That we must bind thee down and clench thy fetters here?'

The opening, with its wintry visitant, is reminiscent of Heathcliff's invocation to the dead Catherine at the beginning of
Wuthering Heights ('Cathy, do come!'). While the six stanzas in
which 'Rochelle' describes her 'liberation' are not at all pre-
Raphaelite, they are Emily Brontë's most challenging statement,
not 'mysticism', but an account of an ecstatic experience with
remarkable symptoms.

'Then dawns the Invisible, the Unseen its truth reveals;
My outward sense is gone, my inward essence feels –
Its wings are almost free, its home, its harbour found;
Measuring the gulf it stoops and dares the final bound!

'Oh, dreadful is the check – intense the agony
When the ear begins to hear and the eye begins to see;
When the pulse begins to throb, the brain to think again
The soul to feel the flesh and the flesh to feel the chain!

This report has many characteristics of the 'classic' ecstatic
experience of the religious mystics, such as unified consciousness
('my inward essence'), transitoriness and pain, though the description is not in orthodox terms. In recent years psychologists have
paid considerable attention to mysticism. They treat it with
respect. To quote a recent summary: 'its validity as a religious

expression is in no way disturbed by psychological investigation'.[14] The ecstatic experience has been connected both with the Ego – or individuality – development, and with regression to the Id, or undifferentiated energy of the psyche, in other words with a retreat from maturity. Even the more sympathetic psychological approaches to ecstasy tend to connect it with, in technical terms, 'the acceptable residue of infantile behaviour'. A suggested connection between such 'oceanic' feelings and the 'primal unity with the mother' is interesting in Emily Brontë's case.[15]

Only the least sceptical approach to mysticism could ignore the striking sexuality of many accounts, including, I think, this one. But this does not mean that it need be considered a form of self-indulgence; rather the reverse, in view of the deprivation needed to attain such states. The conflict of a poem such as 'The Philosopher' and the psychological hinterland Emily Brontë inhabited as poet make 'The Prisoner 'almost predictable (O God within my breast . . .'). One, perhaps too reductive, approach is to compare the ecstatic experience with its many analogues in so-called ordinary life, such as involuntary memory, the effect of drugs, even change of mood. And though resemblances between ecstatic and creative experiences have been pressed into the service of the absolute, by Evelyn Underhill for instance, certain powerful and influential intellectual experiences, the insights of the scientist, have been accompanied by similar states. Emily Brontë's special relationship with the imagination has already taken the form of deification or personification. On the other hand the particular experience described in these lines is not exactly paralleled anywhere in her known work. Some of the greatest women of the nineteenth century – Florence Nightingale, Mrs Browning – left records of influential experiences of a somewhat similar kind.

The problem (as William James recognised) with a record such as this in 'The Prisoner' is that – failing objective measurement – it must be taken on trust, except by other mystics. Mystical writing, it is evident, runs artistic risks akin to the moral dangers (against which orthodoxy often warned) of religious enthusiasm. Emily Brontë succeeds, as she does on the dangerous ground of

Wuthering Heights, because she is as much artist as visionary; she remains observant, with a thread leading back to reality, in which pulses throb. Her monosyllable indeed 'checks' any tendency to over-portentousness. Few writers have given a closer or more impressive record of an extreme imaginative experience. Ecstasy of this order can be considered as the ultimate in romantic hope creating 'from its own wreck the thing it contemplates'. And almost immediately, in this long narrative poem, in the words of Lord Julian, she questions the moment.

Earth's hope was not so dead, heaven's home was not so dear;
I read it in that flash of longing quelled by fear

He sounds like the matter-of-fact Nelly of *Wuthering Heights*. Authentic mysticism among the religious has been distinguished from neurosis by results, and – living in a period of female neurosis – perhaps Emily Brontë can be pronounced saved by works.

V

CHARLOTTE BRONTË'S inspection of one of her sister's two transcript-books, and its consequences, events familiar from her Biographical Notice was at this period, 'in the autumn of 1845'.

something more than surprise seized me – a deep conviction that these were not common effusions, nor at all like the poetry women generally write. I thought them condensed and terse, vigorous and genuine. To my ear they had also a peculiar music – wild, melancholy and elevating.

My sister Emily was not a person of demonstrative character, nor one on the recesses of whose mind and feelings even those nearest and dearest to her could, with impunity, intrude unlicensed; it took hours to reconcile her to the discovery I had made, and days to persuade her that such poems merited publication. I knew, however, that a mind like hers could not be without some latent spark of honourable ambition . . .[1]

She has, perhaps, not had quite sufficient credit for the immediate recognition of their merits, here combined with a certain failure to appreciate the kind of honourable ambition likely to be entertained by her sister. After this confrontation Emily permitted publication of just those poems that most reveal the recesses of her mind and feelings (e.g. 'The Philosopher' and 'The Prisoner'). 'This equivocation', writes J. H. Miller, 'is already present in the fact that she expressed her visions in the language she shared with millions of men.'[2]

Charlotte had long appreciated the strength of her sister's character; she must now have drastically reappraised her as writer. Her letter of 7 October 1845 implies new hope: 'how often does it happen', she wrote Miss Nussey, 'when a hedge of danger and trials seems to enclose us on every side, an opening is suddenly made'.[3] The danger and trials are well known. It was about this time, too, that her increasingly desperate letters to Heger break off.

Emily's manuscripts show that she helped in the work of titling and adapting her poems for the 1846 volume, which includes twenty-one poems, six of them being from the 'Gondal Poems' book. Potentially confusing Gondal traces had to be removed. The notable 'No coward soul is mine' (H191) was not included, being first published in 1850, although, dated 2 January 1846, it presumably could have been. (The joint manuscript was not despatched until early February.) Of all her poems it best shows, perhaps, the 'condensed energy, clearness, finish' of Charlotte's Preface, a directness and disregard of fashion most un-Victorian. Moral conflict, the strife of 'power' and will, the death-wish and rebellious romanticism are excluded. This affirmation of an accessible if undefined deity –

> O God within my breast
> Almighty, ever-present Deity
> Life, that in me hast rest
> As I Undying Life, have power in Thee　　　(H191)

has allowed the orthodox to claim the author, but the import is quite different; the poem forbids any facile interpretation of this kind; there is a shift of stress from dependence on the divine to interdependence.

The line of descent of the attitude here is perhaps from Bruno through Spinoza and German and English romanticism; it is the pantheist feeling for life and nature, the permanent romantic apotheosis of consciousness. 'The power that thinks and works in me is in its nature as eternal as that which holds together the sun and stars.'[4] Herder provides a paraphrase of the poem.

The immediate power, nevertheless, seems to be Shelley. Emily, as noted, was probably familiar with his poetry by 1841. (An echo of an article on Shelley published in *Fraser's Magazine*, June 1838, occurring in *Wuthering Heights* – see below, p. 146 – is also relevant here.) Emily reproduces Shelley's feeling for the perpetuating power of nature as a pledge of some undefined immortality.

> With wide-embracing love
> Thy spirit animates eternal years
> Pervades and broods above,
> Changes, sustains, dissolves, creates and rears
>
> (Spreading itself, where'er that Power may move
> Which has withdrawn his being to its own;
> Which wields the world with never-wearied love,
> Sustains it from beneath, and kindles it above.
>
> *Adonais* XLII)

Her next stanza closely marks the movement of the same poem.

> Though Earth and moon were gone
> And suns and universes ceased to be
> And thou wert left alone
> Every Existence would exist in thee
>
> (The splendours of the firmament of time
> May be eclipsed, but are extinguished not . . . XLIV)

Emily Brontë's poem is nevertheless worthy to be set beside Shelley's. It is not titled in the only manuscript version. Not all her alterations are decipherable, but some are revealing. In the second stanza, quoted above, 'power' is substituted for the original 'strength' – an improvement. The penultimate stanza first read:

> Though Earth and moon were gone
> And suns and universes ceased to shine
> And thou wert left alone
> Every existence would exist in thine

Again, the emphatic 'There is not room for Death' may be compared with the original 'no room'. The poem was published, edited and emasculated by Charlotte in 1850. Amendments to punctuation, such as the substitution of the epistolary dash for Emily Brontë's commas (producing effects like 'As I – undying Life – ', as if undying life were an afterthought) and Charlotte's

'Thou – THOU art Being and Breath' are disastrous. Uniquely among Emily's poems, there are no stops at the end of the stanzas as she wrote it (and as Hatfield scrupulously prints it); it is as if inspiration was too swift for such conventions.

The poem was written during the probable period of writing *Wuthering Heights*. It marks a break, as the last of the 'personal' poems. There is at least a plausible connection between the theme of courage in the poem and its author's attitude to more worldly affairs. Emily had certainly invested some of their money in George Hudson the rail king's York and North Midland line. (Unlikely as it seems – or was it a pledge to fortune – the sisters had each subscribed £1 to a testimonial subscription raised the previous autumn, at a time when Hudson, like an Angrian hero, was entertaining royalty at his Knightsbridge mansion.)[5] What remains of Emily Brontë's account-book confirms yields on the shares of about ten per cent, not unusual at the time of the rail boom, and shows that she apparently invested in more than one company.

Profit from ninety S to H, giving   Share specs   70   6   2
        Total   116 18   4   Total   128 13   9
I exceeded my income by 12   0   0
Besides being answerable for 163 18 10

(Among other entries for 1846 are some petty cash items: 'Collar for F' – their dog Flossy – 'needles' and 'walnuts', and 'Received LM railway coupons, at 10 - 0 - 0'.)[6] *

'S to H' and 'LM' may indicate the Hull and Selby, and Manchester and Leeds lines. The only line, as far as I know, mentioned by Charlotte in her correspondence with Miss Wooler on the subject is the York and North Midland,[7] which does not appear in the remains of the account-book. Rail amalgamation taking place at this time may be the explanation; for instance a bill 'enabling the Hull and Selby Railway Company to Lease and

---

* 'Accounts of receipts and expenditures. Unsigned but in the tiny handprint of Emily J. Brontë . . . top remainders of eleven sheets cut out of a notebook.' Miss M. G. Christian's description (BPM Collection catalogue) helps to explain why my transcription cannot be better than tentative.

also to Sell their railway to the York and N. Midland, and Manchester and Leeds RC or one of them' was advertised, above the name of G. Hudson, in the Press on 27 April 1846.[8]

The poem is dated 2 January 1846, and at the end of the month Charlotte told Miss Wooler that she doubted whether even the best lines could keep up their rate of return, but that Emily did not wish to sell, and was supported by Anne. 'She managed in a most handsome and able manner when I was in Brussels . . . therefore I will let her manage still, and take the consequences. Disinterested and energetic she certainly is', Charlotte wrote, adding that their affection would survive what seemed to her unreasonable and headstrong notions.[9]

Emily's last extant letter was written this spring to Miss Nussey, with whom Charlotte was staying, after negotiating details of publication of the *Poems*.

Dear Miss Nussey, I fancy this note will be too late to decide one way or the other with respect to Charlotte's stay. Yours only came this morning (Wednesday) and unless mine travels faster, you will not receive it till Friday. Papa of course misses Charlotte and will be glad to have her back. Anne and I, ditto; but as she goes from home so seldom you may keep her a day or two longer, if your eloquence is equal to the task of persuading her . . .[10]

Charlotte's correspondence with publishers bears on the problem of the dating of *Wuthering Heights*. (Her sister's communications are lost.) Within nine weeks of first offering the manuscripts of the *Poems* to Aylott and Jones, or by 6 April 1846, she enquired whether they would care to publish a work of fiction by the Bells.[11] Describing their literary début later, in her Biographical Notice, she wrote: 'Ill-success failed to crush us . . . we each set to work on a prose tale.' In fact the *Poems* were not published when fiction was first offered. She showed a similar myth-making tendency when describing 'No coward soul' as her sister's last lines.

The stages, from the various records, are as follows:

'The autumn of 1845'   EB agrees to publication of the poems.

6 April 1846	Sisters prepare for the press a work of fiction.
27 June 1846	Date at the end of MS of CB's *The Professor* (part of the joint MS first submitted).[12]
4 July 1846	The joint MS consisting of *The Professor*, *Wuthering Heights* and *Agnes Grey* submitted to Colburn.[13]
4 August 1846	*The Professor*, with or without the other MSS, returned (by ?) to CB in Manchester.[14]

If *Wuthering Heights* was not contemplated before the discovery of its author's poems led to the joint project, this leaves, at the outside, nine months for its production. (There is some evidence that Emily's sisters were turning their attention to fiction in the true sense, if not first drafts of the works published, before the autumn of 1845.) The 1845 birthday notes refer to writing by Emily, but not to novels: she was then 'writing a work on the first Gondal wars', she had 'plenty of work on hand, and writing'. Anne's note merely states that her sister was 'engaged in writing the Emperor Julius' Life . . .' and poetry.

Though periods as far back as 1837 and 1843/4 have been suggested for the writing of *Wuthering Heights*, perhaps the most widely accepted view is that it was only after these July notes, and after Charlotte's inspection of the poems. In other words, that Emily was a reluctant novelist of most unusual energy and industry, rather than a secret novelist of longer standing. Yet *Wuthering Heights*, with its complicated structure and remarkable consistency of detail, is hardly a work likely to have been written in nine months or less. Kathleen Tillotson has suggested that the evidence points to commencement about January 1846 (leaving less than five months), but adds that the character of the work, and its author's circumstances in 1843, as well as the poems of that period, indicate an earlier inception than 1845/6.[15]

Similarities between the poems and *Wuthering Heights* are not very conclusive. It is easier to suppose that Emily temporarily abandoned Gondal – there are no manuscripts of such poems from

October 1845 to September 1846 – than to imagine her living
with such related characters as an 'Augusta' and a Catherine
Earnshaw at once.

The well-known and rather enigmatic poem 'Often rebuked,
yet always back returning' with its ambiguous statement 'I'll
walk where my own nature would be leading' and its suggestion
that the 'shadowy region' was out of favour is worth calling in
evidence, but it is undated.

> To-day, I will seek not the shadowy region;
>   Its unsustaining vastness waxes drear;
> And visions rising, legion after legion,
>   Bring the unreal world too strangely near.
>
> I'll walk, but not in old heroic traces,
>   And not in paths of high morality,
> And not among the half-distinguished faces
>   The clouded forms of long-past history.
>
> I'll walk where my own nature would be leading:
>   It vexes me to choose another guide:
> Where the gray flocks in ferny glens are feeding;
>   Where the wild wind blows on the mountain side.
>
> What have those lonely mountains worth revealing?
>   More glory and more grief than I can tell:
> The earth that wakes *one* human heart to feeling
>   Can centre both the worlds of Heaven and Hell.

Is this a form of literary notebook entry? (The poem was chosen
by Charlotte for the 1850 selection, and there is no manuscript.
Hatfield suggests that Charlotte herself wrote it, and included
it in this edition, in the preparation of which she took so many
editorial liberties.) Certainly it is odd that this very 'personal'
poem does not appear in Emily Brontë's transcript-book. If it is
by Charlotte, then she rose far above her usual level as poet:
to me the signs are that it is by Emily.

In her account of the Brontës in 1846 in the *Life*, Mrs Gaskell
describes their evening fiction workshop, evidently as Charlotte

described it to her. 'Once or twice each read to the others what she had written, and heard what they had to say about it. Charlotte told me that the remarks seldom had any effect in inducing her to alter her work . . .'[16] 'Often rebuked', if indeed the poem is by Emily, could be, in part, an allusion to such a debate.

Poems by Currer, Ellis and Acton Bell was published in May 1846. The first 'Books Received' notice I have come across is in *Hood's Magazine* for June. By early July, when the first by no means unfavourable reviews were appearing, the joint manuscript of fiction was sent to Henry Colburn. The accounts of the submission and acceptance of the novels given by Charlotte and by Mrs Gaskell do not quite agree. (Despite the confident statements of certain biographers, it is not clear just when Newby *did* accept *Wuthering Heights* and *Agnes Grey*, or whether these two were at any time submitted in a separate package to that of *The Professor*.)

Emily is rarely mentioned in the correspondence until her last illness. She went with her sister on her visit to Manchester (about 2 August 1846) to find an oculist for their father, but did not remain there.[17] Shortly before, Charlotte told Ellen Nussey that she wished they had £50, with which to set off *en masse* to the seaside. 'We could all do with recreation.'[18] This was an understatement. Though we know how Emily Brontë left *Wuthering Heights*, how it left her can only be imagined.

The state of the manuscript of her last poem does indeed raise the question of her health at this time. Although 'Why ask to know the date – the clime?' is somewhat unlike previous work, this – on the face of it – surprising return to the earlier world perhaps provides its own explanation.

> And I confess that hate of rest,
> And thirst for things abandoned now,
> Had weaned me from my country's breast
> And brought me to that land of woe.　　　　(H192)

It is at least possible that this poem, commenced, according to its dating, on 14 September 1846, is not unconnected with her recent visit to the problem city of the 1840s, the focus of concern and apprehension over the condition of the people, the Manchester of Mrs Gaskell's *North and South*. The poem was continued until some time before May 1848, the date on a further draft fragment; in other words the second draft is dated after publication of *Wuthering Heights*. Emily Brontë's first line is an injunction not to look too closely into the exact circumstances of this poem, which is clearly less concerned with Gondal than with the real world and human nature, which it reflects more directly than other Gondal poems. It represents a move towards maturity and responsibility. Like some anonymous piece of news film it plunges the reader into the confusion of civil war. ('The Royalists are not quite overcome', wrote Anne Brontë a year earlier.) The narrator may well be the 'Julian' of 'The Prisoner'. In this poem, a sad reminder of genius unfulfilled, her concern with the social theme is evident.

> Why ask to know the date – the clime?
> More than mere words they cannot be:
> Men knelt to God, and worshipped crime,
> And crushed the helpless, even as we.

Reminders of the 'sultry month' of August in the exceptional summer of 1846 are further evidence of the documentary aspect of the poem.

> Day after day, from noon to noon,
> The August sun blazed bright as June.

> But we with unregarding eyes
> Saw panting earth and glowing skies . . .

(I quote here from the later, 1848 draft.) It is noteworthy that these four-stressed couplets, with a new urgency, suggest the influence of Shelley's *The Mask of Anarchy*, 'Written on the Occasion of the Late Massacre in Manchester'.

> It was the autumn of the year,
> The time to labouring peasants dear;
> Week after week, from noon to noon,
> September shone as bright as June –

Still, never hand a sickle held;
The crops were garnered in the field –
Trod out and ground by horses' feet
While every ear was milky sweet;
And kneaded on the threshing-floor
With mire of tears and human gore.

She was evidently under no illusions as to revolutionary or freedom wars, but individual remorse almost obliterates the narrative
of this long poem. The cause was possibly the situation of her
now rejected brother.

When kindred strive – God help the weak!
A brother's ruth 'tis vain to seek:
At first, it hurt my chivalry
To join them in their cruelty . . .

A sister's ruth, perhaps? The open severity of Charlotte Brontë's
condemnation of her brother at this period has been an issue for
various biographers.

The manuscript is a complete contrast to the usual compact
neatness: it contains many erasures, and the writing tends to
sprawl. At one page the notebook was closed with the ink wet. If
Emily was ill by the early summer of 1847, she successfully con-
cealed it from the rest of the family. (It is not, of course, certain
just how long she was engaged on this poem.) There is a reference
to an outing at this time, to meet Ellen Nussey. 'Emily, Anne
and I', Charlotte wrote, 'will all three meet you at the station.
We can take tea jovially together at the Devonshire Arms.'[19]

Emily's recommencement of 'Why ask to know', a torso of 25
lines, is dated 13 May 1848, or only some six months before her
death. At this date, too, there was no lack of reminders of politics:
her sister had recently been discussing in her letters the flight of
Louis-Philippe and Guizot, and the Chartist agitation in London.[20] The poem breaks off on a note of pessimism. Her final
reproof seems to be aimed at the superficial piety of her age.

Shedders of blood, shedders of tears:
Self-cursers avid of distress;
Yet mocking heaven with senseless prayers
For mercy on the merciless.   (H193)

It is Emily Brontë at her most un-Victorian. The greater part, perhaps all the first draft, of this poem must have been written while *Wuthering Heights* was still looking for a publisher. (This circumstance was the *cause* of the 'thirst for things abandoned now' according to Miss Ratchford and others.) Mrs Gaskell wrote that the book was 'awaiting Newby's pleasure during all the months of early summer'.[21] Though, as mentioned, the date of acceptance of *Wuthering Heights* is difficult to establish, her evidence here agrees with Charlotte's account.

The correspondence relating to the transaction and the identity of the first 'reader' of *Wuthering Heights* are also lost, though details of the former emerged later. Thomas Cautley (sometimes printed 'Cantly') Newby's list included the O'Haras, Lady Lytton, G. P. R. James and – briefly – Anthony Trollope. Certainly an opportunist, he was more than the swagman of the book trade described by many Brontë biographers. He is on record[22] as a noted publisher of fiction, but this is not borne out by Michael Sadleir, who has stated that Newby's authors were either new and unknown, or old and in decline, and that he traded in remainder sheets. Lady Lytton's publishers, he adds, were all second-rate, their sales organisation, publicity and production standards poor[23] – all shortcomings that may have affected the reception of *Wuthering Heights*. G. P. R. James, according to Sadleir, was 'reduced' to being published by Newby.[24]

In 1843 Newby appears at 65 Mortimer Street, Cavendish Square; by 1846 at number 72, and by 1850 at the better address of 30 Welbeck Street, where he remained until his retirement in 1875. He described himself in the directories and in prelims of his books as both publisher and bookseller (as was usual) and sometimes also as printer.

His dealings with the Brontës have not enhanced his reputation. Some details of his agreement with Emily and Anne Brontë emerged when their sister was discussing the memorial edition with Smith, Elder. It provided for 350 copies of the three-decker novel (2 volumes *Wuthering Heights*, 1 volume *Agnes Grey*), the sisters advancing £50 ('terms somewhat impoverishing') and evidently included an option on future works. Charlotte mentioned that

a sale of 250 copies (presumably at the usual 31s 6d) should leave
a surplus of £100 to be divided.

> No portion of the sum advanced has yet been returned, and as
> it appears that the work is now entirely out of print, I should
> feel greatly obliged if you would call on Mr Newby and enquire
> whether it would be convenient to refund the amount . . .[25]

Six months before the probable date of acceptance of *Wuthering
Heights*, Newby offered 'half-profits' terms to Frances Trollope,
who was negotiating for her son's first novel, an arrangement
which Trollope disliked. 'He [i.e. Newby], like everyone else,
gives a most wretched account of the novel market.'[26]

Newby promised, but failed to supply, a statement of the sales
of *Wuthering Heights* (Trollope's experience was the same[27]) and
threatened action for copyright when Smith, Elder proposed to
publish it. He claimed to have lost on it, and Charlotte abandoned
her attempt to recover the money put up by her sisters.[28] The
condition of the first edition of *Wuthering Heights* and *Agnes Grey*
supports Sadleir's comment on Newby's standards of production.
'The books are not well got up', Charlotte reported, ' – They
abound in errors of the press.'[29]

From early 1848 the public existence of the Bells, and soon of
the Brontës, was very real, but Ellis Bell (as might be expected)
did all she could to avoid becoming Emily Brontë to the world.
At this period more than ever she must be seen through other's
eyes. Occasional reports of her manifest the usual 'containment'
(as Ellen Nussey put it). In the previous autumn Charlotte had
been to visit her friend.

> Emily is just now sitting on the floor of the bedroom where I am
> writing, looking at her apples. She smiled when I gave them
> and the collar to her as your presents, with an expression at
> once well-pleased and slightly surprised.[30]

In October 1847 Anne (then writing *The Tenant of Wildfell Hall*)
had complained of the wind. 'Emily considers it a very uninteresting wind, but it does not affect her nervous system.'[31] There
are no more than similar glimpses of her response to the reception of *Wuthering Heights*. There was, it seems to me, sufficient

praise in even the earliest reviews to console for the injury of the more hostile, though the Brontës' sensitivity to charges of coarseness must be estimated with a Victorian rather than a modern outlook. Emily almost certainly saw several notices, in addition to those her sister mentions in her letters; they were among the most favourable. Cuttings from the *Examiner*, and less prestigious journals – the *Atlas*, *Britannia*, and *Douglas Jerrold's Magazine* – were found in her folding writing-case. This in itself does not prove she saw them, since this relic-to-be was not, of course, sealed at her death, and many things found after it was sold were not in fact hers.[32]

During 1848, at first behind her *nom de plume*, Charlotte Brontë enjoyed her widening circle, and fast became something of a Victorian sage, in continuous correspondence with her publishers and less frequently with authors such as Lewes and Thackeray. A letter to W. S. Williams, the reader for Smith, Elder, shows the usual tolerant, affectionate disagreement with her sister, and a glimpse of the pastoralist author of *Wuthering Heights*. 'Ellis', she wrote, 'will not be seen in his full strength till he is seen as an essayist.'

I do not think he admits it as his creed that 'the proper study of mankind is man' – at least not the artificial man of cities. In some points I consider Ellis somewhat of a theorist: now and then he broaches ideas which strike my sense as more daring and original than practical; his reason may be in advance of mine but certainly it often travels a different road.[33]

Emily presumably would not have accompanied her sisters on their celebrated visit to London in early July 1848 even if domestic responsibilities (an infirm father, and brother within weeks of his death) had been less pressing.

Permit me to caution you [Charlotte wrote Williams afterwards] not to speak of my sisters when you write to me. I mean do not use the word in the plural. Ellis Bell will not endure to be alluded to under any other appellation than the 'nom de plume'. I committed a grand error in betraying his identity to you and Mr Smith. It was inadvertent – the words 'we are three sisters' escaped me . . .[34]

Emily's influence here extends even over her sister's grammar. 'His' identity was already known, but the letter shows how strongly she resented any further reference to it.

It has often been suggested that she was writing or considering another work at this time. There is a well-known letter dated in early February 1848 from Newby, fitting an envelope addressed to 'Ellis Bell', and referring to another novel in progress.[35] The work in question may well in fact have been Anne's *The Tenant of Wildfell Hall*, soon to be published. There is some evidence that, apart from intentional confusion, Newby was not clear about the identities of his authors. He advertised *Wuthering Heights* as 'Acton Bell's successful new novel' in January 1848. His advertising is revealing in other respects. In *Douglas Jerrold's Magazine* (5 February 1848) he took space for *Wuthering Heights*, 'By The Successful New Novelist', an evident attempt to connect it with the fame of *Jane Eyre*. In the *Examiner* (19 February) it was 'Mr Bell's successful new novel'. In the same journal (5 and 12 August 1848) in letters to the Editor, he tried to justify his practice of using quotations from the Glasgow *Examiner* and Manchester *Examiner* as if from the London *Examiner*. Among the hints of a second work by Emily, however, there is Charlotte's inconclusive 'They were both prepared to try again' of her Biographical Notice to the 1850 *Wuthering Heights*.[36] The sort of novel Emily might have written to follow *Wuthering Heights* is far from obvious.

Legendary elements, as with the death of Emily herself, cling to the end of Branwell Brontë on 24 September 1848. (Not much is reliably known about the relationship between Branwell and Emily, but it is reasonably certain that *Wuthering Heights* and Heathcliff would hardly have been the same without this example of romantic self-destruction so close to its author.) The 'quite uninteresting wind' blew again at the funeral, and shortly after (9 October) Emily was reported as having a cough and cold. Pulmonary tuberculosis may be well advanced before the sufferer realises the seriousness of his condition. Now, for the first time, she takes a permanent and central place in the letters. Cough, emaciation and fever caused her family concern, but the situation deepened her reserve. 'It is useless to question her; you get no answers. It is still more useless to recommend remedies; they are never adopted.'[37] Charlotte as letter-writer now takes her due place also as Victorian domestic tragedian. In early November Emily was struggling through her normal household routine.[38] Ten days before her death she was sitting up for fifteen hours a day.[39] George Smith attempted to cheer the household with parcels of books.

> I think a certain harshness in her peculiar and powerful nature [Charlotte wrote] makes me cling to her more. But all this is family egotism (so to speak) – excuse it, and, above all, never allude to it, or to the name Emily when you write to me.[40]

At the end of November Charlotte read her the notice of *Wuthering Heights* in the *North American Review*. It was partly unfavourable, and confused as to the authorship of the novels.

> I studied the two ferocious authors, Ellis, the 'man of uncommon talents, but dogged, brutal and morose' sat leaning back in his easy-chair drawing his impeded breath as best he could, and looking, alas! piteously pale and wasted; it is not his wont to laugh, but he smiled, half-amused and half in scorn as he listened.[41]

Charlotte's advisers in London were more familiar with the forbidden identity of Ellis Bell than Ellis herself knew. They urged Charlotte to persuade her to submit to the homoeopathy then fashionable. She was shown the letters: Mr Williams's intention was kind, 'but he was under a delusion. Homoeopathy was only another form of quackery.'[42] She was not quite correct. It has affinities with inoculation. But effective chemotherapy and sanatorium treatment for consumption were still years ahead. Charlotte tried to face the prospect of her death.

> She is *very* ill. I believe, if you were to see her, your impression would be that there is no hope. A more hollow, wasted, pallid aspect I have not beheld. The deep, tight cough continues; the breathing after the least exertion is a rapid pant; and these symptoms are accompanied by pains in the chest and side. Her pulse, the only time she allowed it to be felt, was found to beat 115 per minute. In this state she resolutely refuses to see a

doctor; she will not give an explanation of her feelings, she will scarcely allow her illness to be alluded to.[43]

Emily's behaviour, about which there has been so much speculation, of course fits no ordinary clinical pattern (though TB cases are sometimes said to be pathologically and necessarily difficult). Psychiatrists sometimes need to abolish distinctions between real and fantasy events, and though here the case is different, being one of an actual threat to physical existence, it seems to me there is abundant evidence in her work and life to explain her behaviour, evidence of her belief in the will, in nature, and of her unviolated isolation. Also, perhaps, of her desire for death. Her behaviour was possibly as near suicide as the tenets of her milieu allowed her to get. In a sense, as on some other occasions, dare one suggest, she tried to have it both ways. A great deal of hocus-pocus and general nastiness was involved in Victorian popular belief about treatment of illness as is evident from the many household reference books; one, Graham's *Modern Domestic Medicine*, was in the house. A sensitive and sceptical person may well have been reluctant to submit to such attentions.

In early December she read Dr Curie on homoeopathy, sent by Williams, but refused to attempt the treatment.[44] By 9 December her sister was more hopeful that she would consent to homoeopathy, which would involve no violation of her privacy.[45] Charlotte wrote, via Williams, to Dr Epps, an authority. Her letter is the last detailed portrait.

The patient, respecting whose case Dr Epps is consulted and for whom his opinion and advice are requested is a female in her 29th year [in fact her 31st]. A peculiar reserve of character renders it difficult to draw from her all the symptoms of her malady, but as far as they can be ascertained they are as follows:
Her appetite failed; she evinced a continual thirst, with a craving for acids, and required a constant change of beverage. In appearance she grew rapidly emaciated; her pulse – the only time she allowed it to be felt, was found to be 115 per minute. The patient usually appeared worse in the forenoon, she was then exhausted and drowsy; towards evening she was often better.

Expectoration accompanies the cough. The shortness of breath is aggravated by the slightest exertion. The patient's sleep is supposed to be tolerably good at intervals, but disturbed by paroxysms of coughing. Her resolution to contend against illness being very fixed, she has never consented to lie in bed for a single day – she sits up from 7 in the morning until 10 at night. All medical aid she has rejected, insisting that Nature should be left to take her own course. She has taken no medicine, but occasionally a mild aperient and Lococks cough wafers, of which she has used about 3 per diem, and considers their effect very beneficial. Her diet, which she regulates herself, is very simple and light.

The patient has hitherto enjoyed pretty good health, though she has never looked strong, and the family constitution is not supposed to be robust. Her temperament is highly nervous. She has been accustomed to a sedentary and studious life.

If Dr Epps can, from what has here been stated, give an opinion on the case, and prescribe a course of treatment, he will greatly oblige the patient's friends.

Address – Miss Brontë, Parsonage, Haworth, Bradford, Yorks.[46]

Dr Epps can have been in little doubt of the outcome. His opinion, Charlotte wrote, was expressed 'too obscurely to be of use'. (Hippocrates advised doctors to avoid patients in the later stages of phthisis, in case their reputations should suffer.)

Curst be he who moves the bones of one of the strangest and most legendary events in English literary biography. But the story of Emily Brontë's death has, perhaps, been influenced by contemporary attitudes to death, by Victorian solemnity and love of sentimental trappings. Mrs Gaskell's account of her rising as usual on her last morning, of the collapse of her resolution not to see a doctor, of her failure to recognise a sprig of heather specially sought by her sister, is more colourful than verifiable.[47] The last detail, for instance, can be found in many literary deaths of the period, while Mrs Gaskell's account of the doctor incident is almost certainly incorrect.

She misinterprets the letters she uses in her biography. Charlotte's letter to Dr Epps becomes, in the *Life*, an actual visit from a doctor whom Emily refuses to see.

When a doctor had been sent for, and was in the very house Emily refused to see him. Her sisters could only describe to him what symptoms they had observed; and the medicines which he sent she would not take, denying that she was ill.[48]

This seems to be based on Charlotte's letter to Ellen Nussey: 'The physician's opinion was expressed too obscurely to be of use. He sent some medicines which she would not take.'[49] It refers, of course, to Dr Epps. Why, if he really was 'in the very house', should he send medicines?

The heather incident was related to her, Mrs Gaskell states, by Charlotte herself; nevertheless it has all the appearance of a Victorian deathbed motif.[50] Her account of the last morning, when Emily is described as rising as usual, and allowing no one to help her, was obtained from the servant Martha Brown. The horsehair sofa on which Emily is said to have died is a later detail, and seems to have no basis in the records. It is quite possible, however, that A. M. F. Robinson, writing her *Emily Brontë* later in the century, had access to reminiscences which may be true.

In the light of Severn's terrible account of Keats's death from the same complaint, an interesting comparison in taste with Victorian deathbeds, one might think that a patient in the last stages of consumption could not do what Emily is said to have done. On the other hand, even medical opinion will not be committed as to what exceptional human beings could or could not do in these circumstances.

Charlotte's references to the event do not confirm the legend. Haunted by it, she often referred to it in rather stylised terms. On her return from Scarborough after Anne's death she wrote to Williams, mentioning 'Emily's large house-dog, which lay at the side of her *dying bed*'[51] (my italics). She evidently had the same occasion in mind when referring, in 1852, to the death of Ellen Taylor in New Zealand, in a letter to Ellen Nussey. 'It ripped up half-scarred wounds with terrible force. The death-bed was just the same.'[52]

Little more is known from the Brontës themselves. On Monday, 18 December 1848 Charlotte read to Emily from Emerson's essays, sent by Smith, Elder Ltd, 'I read on till I found she was not listening.'[53] Next morning she wrote the letter quoted, about Dr Epps's advice, to Ellen Nussey. Emily died a few hours afterwards, after a 'short, hard conflict'.[54] 'I cannot forget Emily's death-day', she wrote early in 1849, 'it becomes a more fixed, a darker, a more frequently recurring idea in my mind than ever; it was very terrible . . .'[55] 'Turning her dying eyes', she wrote, 'from the pleasant sun . . .'[56] An intense feeling for life is implicit in Emily's best work, but one wonders whether she wished to prolong life itself. She was buried in Haworth church on Friday, 22 December 1848. Not all the legend need be questioned. Her dog, Charlotte wrote, 'followed her funeral to the vault, lying in the pew couched at our feet while the burial service was being read'.[57] The *Bradford Observer*, 21 December, published an inaccurate notice of her death.

Same day, in the 29th year of her age, Emily Jane, daughter of the Rev. P. Brontë, of Haworth.

BOOK TWO
Wuthering Heights

1. 'Epic' into Image: *Wuthering Heights* and the Gondal poems

ONLY a month or so before the three Brontës decided to submit novels for publication, Emily was still deeply involved with Gondal. 'We intend sticking firmly by the rascals', i.e. the Gondal characters, she wrote in 1845. (It was a declaration more appropriate to her own interest than to Anne's.) The poems show that she remained loyal while *Wuthering Heights* was being submitted for publication and even after the book had appeared. The 'thirst for things abandoned now' of an 1846 poem may be an inexplicit reference to Gondal, and the poem itself shows that Gondal was not at that time abandoned. There is a great deal in the prose notes about Gondal, nothing about *Wuthering Heights*.

The writer who now produced her first novel was, on the evidence, an assiduous poet drawn to take part in a joint project. It would be surprising if *Wuthering Heights* itself did not reflect the transition, and critics[1] soon noticed the special relationship. The poems in Emily Brontë's Gondal transcript-book are grouped according to characters, such as Augusta, Julius and Lord Alfred, and Miss M. Visick[2] has suggested that this indicates a deliberate marshalling of aspects of Gondal characters with a view to the creation of a new set of fictional characters. If this is so, then Emily Brontë's intention to write a novel would have to be dated back to early 1844 – a good deal earlier than the main evidence suggests. But there are plenty of other and perhaps better reasons for such grouping of poems by character.

Miss Ratchford[3] has found that the Gondal poems show *Wuthering Heights* 'in the making'. This, it seems to me, is just what they do not show. The similarities do, however, suggest the palaeontological relationship between a crude organism and a highly

developed one. When Emily Brontë wrote about the 'unsustaining
vastness' of the 'shadowy region' she may well have been allud-
ing to Gondal. Indeed, its very vastness seems to have influenced
Wuthering Heights in that it presented problems that called for the
particular form of the novel for their solution. The relationship
would, of course, be much less interesting if *Wuthering Heights* were
an ordinary novel. It could be taken as showing a certain narrow-
ness in a novelist; on the other hand it is evidence of the con-
tinuity and depth of Emily Brontë's concerns.

No detailed reconstruction of the Gondal story or stories is
needed to provide illustration of the connection. Such reconstruc-
tions have already been attempted with great ingenuity and per-
severance, but without much solid success. Even summary
examples indicate how the poems amplify understanding of the
ideas and beliefs underlying the novel. (I. H. Buchen has defined
some of them very interestingly in his paper 'Emily Brontë and the
Metaphysics of Childhood and Love'.)

Central in both Gondal poems and *Wuthering Heights* is the theme
of infidelity; it was obsessional, the necessary opposite to an idealised view of human relationships in which love is sufficient to
make mankind independent of God. Love is a challenge to heaven
itself. In 'A.G.A., The Death of' (H143) the obscure characters
Angelica and Douglas are plotting Augusta's assassination because
she has taken Angelica's lover, and then deserted him.

> First made her love his only stay,
> Then snatched the treacherous prop away.

Augusta's is a history of infidelity, exemplified in 'Light up thy
halls!', 'Thou standest in the greenwood now' and 'Written in the
Gaaldine Prison Caves to A.G.A.' (H85, 110 and 133), the
sufferers being Fernando and Alfred. And in 'Song by J. Brenzaida' (H81) the singer has suffered from Geraldine's infidelity
before himself deserting her.

The *Wuthering Heights* relationships are more fully anticipated in
several poems. Augusta, Rosina of Ancona (singer of 'Cold in the
earth' and the less familiar 'Weeks of wild delirium past') and
A. G. Rochelle (of 'Silent is the house') all show aspects of Cather-

ine Earnshaw: her admiration for the heroic, her sense of the transcendent, her remorse, her conflicting impulses, the response of the calmer side of her nature to the mild, Edgar-like Lord Alfred.

> Then art thou not my golden June
> All mist and tempest free? (H137)

The poems reveal, like *Wuthering Heights*, a world governed by certain definite laws. It generates its own evil, which begets further evil. Less justly, passionate intensity has to be paid for in suffering.

> Bliss like thine is bought by years
> Dark with torment and with tears. (H112)

Many poems reflect the wild, God-and-Nature-defying childhood of characters resembling Heathcliff and Catherine, and their separation. For instance the two songs by Julius Brenzaida (H80–81) and 'The soft unclouded blue of air' (H99)

> No; that tree with branches riven,
> Whitening in the whirl of snow,
> As it tossed against the heaven,
> Sheltered happy hearts below – (H80)

A connection between Brenzaida, the warrior of obscure origin and republican leader, and Heathcliff is suggested by several poems in which he is not named. Fulfilment denied results in violence.

> That iron man was born like me,
> And he was once an ardent boy . . .
>
> Oh, crime can make the heart grow old
> Sooner than years of wearing woe;
> Can turn the warmest bosom cold
> As winter wind or polar snow. (H99)

The 'iron man' is forged by crime, or, as a foundling, he is the offspring of evil, both of which circumstances call to mind the early life of Heathcliff. And if he and Brenzaida are the same, then the latter's role as republican leader is a more explicit fictional expression of the social theme, which, it has been suggested, is implicit in the figure of Heathcliff.

Certainly the bleak eponymous island of Gondal, inhabited by a 'royal race', and its southern dependency of Gaaldine seem to prefigure the setting for the action of the novel. There is the same moral premium on the harsh and the austere.

> What flower in Ula's gardens sweet
> Is worth one flake of snow?   (H166)

(The thought comes from an associate of the band of young companions, the 'Unique Society' mentioned in Anne's 1845 prose note.)

Miss M. Visick and Miss Van Ghent[4] have discussed the teasing connection between the two enigmatic poems 'H.A. and A.S.' and 'A.E. and R.C.' and *Wuthering Heights*. 'H.A. and A.S.' seems to describe an encounter with a ghost.

> And if he came not for her woe,
> He would not now return;
> He would not leave his sleep below
> When she had ceased to mourn.   (H153)

More interestingly, the pair are re-enacting an earlier situation, the male figure here appears to have descended from the female of a former encounter.

> And only *he* had locks of light,
>   And *she* had raven hair;
> While now, his curls are dark as night,
> And hers as morning fair.

These transposed contrasts call to mind similar contrasts in *Wuthering Heights*: that of the fair Catherine and dark Heathcliff, Nelly Dean's reconciliatory and symbolic twisting together of a lock of Edgar Linton's hair with one of Heathcliff's, and Lockwood's description of the second Catherine and Hareton. 'Its owner stood behind her, her light shining ringlets blending at intervals with his brown locks' (ch. XXXII).

The pattern is repeated, with an explicit statement of the theme of redemption, in a later poem 'A.E. and R.C.', in which the strophe and antistrophe describe how a 'child of delight, with sunbright hair' takes upon herself (or himself) the 'gloomy sadness' of a melancholy boy.

> I, the image of light and gladness,
> Saw and pitied that mournful boy,
> And I swore to take his gloomy sadness,
> And give to him my beamy joy.   (H187)

Taken together, the earlier and the later poems are irresistibly reminiscent of the way in which the dark essence of the Earnshaws in Hareton is accepted and redeemed by the love of Catherine. (Even if one knew the names of the characters indicated by initials in the headings of these poems, it would not necessarily elucidate the Gondal story. 'H.A.' could be the Henry Angora, mentioned in Emily Brontë's 1845 prose note.) Reading the poems for their connection with *Wuthering Heights*, Dorothy Van Ghent[5] finds a symbolic pattern, which is disturbed in the action of the novel and which re-forms at the end, a process during which, however, something valuable is lost.

With Cathy and Hareton Earnshaw, her cousin on her mother's side, the 'two children' are again in their right relationship of golden and dark, and now the pathos of the dark child cures the daemon out of the golden one, and the maternal care of the golden child raises the dark one to civilised humanity, and makes him a proper husband.

The point is, perhaps, that the object, the desired state of affairs, is not a matter of redemption or conversion in the religious sense, but a mutual one of fulfilment. The pattern may have originated in the Brontës' reaction to the absolutism, the 'black and white' of Calvinist ideas.

'Written in Aspin Castle' (H154) appears to be related to the poems I have been discussing. Evidently spoken by a subsidiary character in the story, the poem is like an unwritten sequel to *Wuthering Heights*, a superfluous episode in which a character resembling Edgar haunts a place rather similar to Thrushcross Grange. The love of the mild Lord Alfred, the 'first chief of Aspin grey', for 'Sidonia's deity' (probably Augusta) resulted in

his moral destruction. The hall of the castle contains their portraits
and their daughter's.

> The hall is full of portraits rare;
> Beauty and mystery mingle there:
> At his right hand an infant fair
> Looks from its golden frame;
> And just like his its ringlets bright,
> Its large dark eye of shadowy light,
> Its cheeks' pure hue, its forehead white,
> And like its noble name.

On one of Emily's poetry manuscripts (Hatfield D8) there is a
list of names, with personal details in codified form:

Flora, 17 June 18th B 5–6 Chesnut [*sic*] H – brown E – GN –
R&W – F

Flora is one of the little band mentioned in the poem 'Companions, all day long we've stood' (H141). The abbreviated details
evidently refer to her appearance: 'Chesnut H(air) – brown E(yes)
– G(reek) [or G(ondal)] N(ose) – (Red) & W(hite complexion)',
etc.[6] The features of the 'infant fair' in 'Aspin Castle' are
described in much the same order, and the mysterious list may be
connected with such a portrait gallery, or be a register. (Flora makes
only these two brief appearances.) The situation in the poem seems
to be connected with the Linton family in the novel. The appearance of the portraits in moonlight is described, just like those of
Edgar Linton and Catherine (who destroyed his life) which hang
on the walls of the Grange. 'We had not yet lighted a candle, but
all the apartment was visible, even to the portraits on the wall –
the splendid head of Mrs Linton and the graceful one of her
husband' (ch. XXIX). In 'Aspin Castle', then, the Gondal counter-
parts of characters in *Wuthering Heights* are present in a setting
strikingly similar to that of an episode in the novel. (Miss Van
Ghent has helped understanding of the operation of the image of the
enclosure or frame, whether of closet bed, coffin, window, or paint-
ing, as dividing states of mind and of existence, in Emily Brontë's
work.) There are many other situations in the poems similar to
those of the novel, though perhaps none as detailed as this.

The reappearance of Gondal in *Wuthering Heights* as metaphor also, is consistent with a process of concentration and re-creation. 'A. G. Rochelle' describes her mystical experience as a prisoner in the poem so called, and Catherine in the novel says, 'The thing that irks me most is this shattered prison, after all . . .' Lockwood observes that Hareton's bearing was 'free, almost haughty', suggesting that this debased member of the emotional aristocracy, the Earnshaws, had an aristocratic counterpart in Gondal. He remarks to Nelly Dean, 'Nay, if it made me a king I'd not be scorned for seeking her good will.' The foundling Heathcliff's relationship to the emperor Julius perhaps shows when Nelly tells him, 'You're fit for a prince in disguise. Who knows but what your father was emperor of China, and your mother an Indian queen.' (There are, of course, similar connections between characters in Charlotte's novels and the 'burning clime' of her early writing.)

It has been suggested[7] that Augusta, Rosina, Rochelle and so on are different names for a single character. This might be thought improbable in the work of a writer who set such store by identity in names and who conceived her characters (as we have seen) in close detail; but the problem is not a serious one. A series of characters with separate names but similar characteristics are, in a sense, a single character. (W. D. Paden has suggested that to approach Gondal via *Wuthering Heights* may be risky.[8]) Both worlds have a strongly dynastic flavour. The early reviewers of *Wuthering Heights*, without benefit of our long familiarity with the book, found it necessary to draw up family trees for the characters, and the practice survives in some editions. Gondal characters such as 'Julius Angora' or 'Sidonia's deity' are known by their titles as well as by their names; and where the relationships between the characters in *Wuthering Heights* become most involved, for instance in the sections describing Heathcliff's abduction of the young Catherine and her forced marriage to his son, Linton Heathcliff, names and titles are confusing in the same way. There is nothing unusual in Heathcliff being referred to as 'her father in law' (ch. XXIX) just as a reminder, but later the second Catherine is referred to as 'Mrs Linton' by the maid, Zillah, when she relates

events to Mrs Dean. She is, in fact, Mrs Heathcliff, and if not
an isolated instance of a slip on the author's part, this mode of
address must be an affectionate form for ' Mrs Linton Heathcliff'
to avoid confusion with the first Mrs Heathcliff, who has recently
died. Again, Catherine II is (correctly) addressed as 'Mrs Heathcliff' a little later. Hareton is sometimes 'Mr Hareton' and sometimes 'Earnshaw' his 'landed title'.

Evidently, though *Wuthering Heights* is not to be found 'in the
making' in Gondal, the preoccupations of the mind that created
it are felt everywhere. No other Victorian novel (perhaps no other
novel) is related to the author's work from childhood in quite this
way.

The new work condenses and selects material from the earlier:
related but separate characters are fused into individuals, and
external details become metaphor. Supernatural happenings in
Gondal cease to belong to a non-mimetic realm, but are used
more subtly, to hint at the existence of other worlds than this, to
suggest that human experience is at least worthy of a supernatural
dimension.

Both the narrative technique of *Wuthering Heights*, in which his-
toric time is enclosed in and juxtaposed with present time, and
its unusually long time-span (which permits an extension of
consciousness) seem to be connected with its 'epic' origins. The
homely eye-witness and the 'wedding-guest' audience were,
perhaps, an essential solution to the problems of transition posed.
It seems possible too that the unusually consistent control of this
time-span resulted, not only from the capacity of its author's
imagination, but also from her having inhabited Gondal for so
long. *Wuthering Heights* does not, in fact, give a very 'real' impression of time as found in mainstream novelists such as George
Eliot, or Tolstoy or Proust; a certain violence is done to the
'natural' lapse of time. Narrative adroitness cannot quite conceal
that an entire childhood lasts only a paragraph or two. 'Till she
reached the age of thirteen she [young Catherine] had not once
been beyond the range of the park by herself . . .' (ch. XVIII). She
had not had time! A similar arbitrary treatment is apparent in the
Gondal events.

If Gondal enabled Emily Brontë to discover and develop her concerns, artistically she did not work, as has been suggested, *from* Gondal but *away* from it. The events of *Wuthering Heights* take place in a region and society that, however unusual, are vividly, intensely, felt. The wayward and unhappy Gondal's queen becomes Catherine Earnshaw. Realism is a salutary, even moral, influence.

No one, after studying the poems, would expect their author to write *Wuthering Heights*. When Emily Brontë set out to do so, different experience made itself felt. And though an area of the unexplained will, of course, remain, the evidence (such as it is) of that experience, may be worth considering.

2. ' . . . no model but the vision of his meditations'?

THE question-mark is, of course, mine, not Charlotte Brontë's. She implied, in her Preface to *Wuthering Heights*, that her sister was a 'natural' or naïve writer, who conceived her work and the narrative technique with which she presented it in isolation.

With regard to the rusticity of *Wuthering Heights*, I admit the charge, for I feel the quality. It is rustic all through. It is moorish, and wild, and knotty as a root of heath. Nor was it natural that it should be otherwise; the author being herself a native and nursling of the moors. Doubtless, had her lot been cast in a town, her writings, if she had written at all, would have possessed another character. Even had chance or taste led her to choose a similar subject, she would have treated it otherwise. Had Ellis Bell been a lady or gentleman accustomed to what is called 'the world', her view of a remote and unreclaimed region, as well as of the dwellers therein, would have differed greatly from that actually taken by the homebred country girl . . .

. . . Had she but lived, her mind would of itself have grown like a strong tree, loftier, straighter, wider-spreading, and its matured fruits would have attained a mellower ripeness and a sunnier bloom; but on that mind time and experience alone could work; to the influence of other intellects it was not amenable.[1]

The implication is not only that Emily is a 'primitive', but that this quality is undesirable, that it indicates artistic immaturity. (The same accusation was levelled at Blake by some of his contemporaries.) In her letters, Charlotte added to this portrait, which was widely accepted as an accurate one – not surprisingly in view of her privileged position as observer. Her criticisms, too, are felt to be valid by many readers of *Wuthering Heights*. Her account is one side of the question in a fairly long-standing debate about Emily Brontë's self-awareness as a writer and the models, if any, of her art. One must give Charlotte the benefit of the doubt by first recognising that she may have been aware of the sort of qualities in *Wuthering Heights* that have led to more recent accusations of 'immaturity'. (The fact that Emily could return to the creation of Gondal after producing such a work as *Wuthering Heights* could be taken as evidence of lack of self-awareness.)

Nevertheless one can't help feeling that she distorts the portrait in this Preface. The 'homebred country girl' had, after all, spent nearly a year in an excellent continental school. The 'charge' that Charlotte Brontë admits is as much her own as that of the reviewers she imputes it to. The comment that Ellis Bell's view of life would have been different had she been worldly is, of course, true enough, but it misses the point that this view is presented through the eyes of a 'gentleman accustomed to what is called "the world" '. Charlotte's inability or refusal adequately to appreciate the profundity, the psychological truth and evidence of intellect in *Wuthering Heights* is less surprising, perhaps, than the absence in her Preface of any sign of recognition of the capacity for subtle presentation, the concern for design and detail that were part of her sister's equipment. Emily herself, one supposes, did not go any part of the way to help her sister to understand her intentions. An arraignment of Charlotte Brontë as critic would, however, be misplaced here, and one must re- member the circumstances of bereavement in which her prefaces were produced.

Were there indeed no models for *Wuthering Heights*? Certainly not in the sense that would deprive it of its originality and place it in a genre. Opinion is at one on this. Here is a difficult problem, in that the external and internal evidence do not confirm each other and because the general data is so limited. Is the naïve Emily Brontë the reality, and the conscious artist, aware of romantic theory and borrowing the elements she required, con- cealing a relatively wide reading in the literature of her time, a pedantic and sentimental fiction? Charlotte's pronouncements are contradictory. 'In some points I consider Ellis somewhat of a theorist',[2] she wrote to W. S. Williams in 1848. A glance at the evidence – and one must not conclude that borrowing implies conscious use of source-material – can appropriately begin with another observation by Charlotte, from her letter to Dr Epps during her sister's last illness: 'She has been accustomed to a solitary and studious life'; or – with due reservation – with Nelly Dean's 'I have read more than you would fancy, Mr Lockwood' (ch. VII).

The material present in the eddy-currents of romanticism became widely distributed, and the *Zeitgeist* was pervasive, so the identification of 'sources' is at best somewhat tentative. Literary echoes, which are what one must mainly go by here, can be the result of coincidence, and thus as mocking as echoes usually are. (I suspect that the opening of Gerard Manley Hopkins's 'The Windhover' unconsciously echoes the Dauphin's apostrophising of his horse, in Shakespeare's *Henry V*, but who is to say?)

Scott, we know, was among Emily Brontë's first preferences at the age of eleven. (The Brontës had access to a set of Scott's novels in Keighley,[3] in addition to some titles among their own books. They were given the *Tales of a Grandfather* by their aunt.[4]) This is another instance of writers in whom he awoke a new sense of region; he was in the literary air the Brontës breathed from childhood. (The rationalist' influence of Jane Austen out of the eighteenth century they ignored, except perhaps for Anne.)

Scott bequeathed Emily Brontë a feeling for atmosphere, as well, perhaps, as hints of the function of narrators (in some of his informative retainers, such as Jenny Dennison in *Old Mortality*, whose reports help to link the narrative; Thady, in Maria Edgeworth's *Castle Rackrent*, performs a similar function, and provides an ironic viewpoint). A house in *Old Mortality* immediately calls to mind the atmosphere of *Wuthering Heights*.

> Everything, indeed, was in repair; there were no slates deficient upon the steep, grey roof, and no panes broken in the narrow windows. But the grass in the court-yard looked as if the foot of man had not been there for years. ch. XXXIX)

With this one can compare Lockwood's final impressions of Wuthering Heights, left to its ghosts.

> When beneath its walls I perceived decay had made progress, even in seven months – many a window showed black gaps deprived of glass; and slates jutted off, here and there, beyond the right line of the roof, to be gradually worked off in coming autumn storms. (ch. XXXIV)

The hero, Morton, in Scott's novel is instructed to negotiate the maze-like interior of the house, Milnwood, much as old Joseph might direct strangers (such as Lockwood, or Isabella) at Wuthering Heights.

> Then bide a wee bit where ye are, friend – or stay – gang round by the back o' the house, and ye'll find a laigh door; it's on the latch for it's never barred till sunset. Ye'll open it – and tak' care ye dinna fa' ower the tub, for the entry's dark – and then ye'll haul to the right, and then ye'll straight forward . . .
>
> (ch. XXXIX)

Emily Brontë inverts Scott's description – in the first passage quoted – and details of the interior of Wuthering Heights take on greater poetic and symbolic force: doors usually *are* barred, and there are fierce dogs under the dresser. The atmosphere, extravagant speech, use of the supernatural and nomenclature – 'Earnscliff', for instance – of another of Scott's tales, *The Black Dwarf*, with which the young Brontës were certainly familiar, all indicate a work to which Emily was attracted temperamentally (though it is essentially quite unlike *Wuthering Heights*). The character of the wronged laird, Mauley, dominates the story: he is another romantic misanthrope and avenger, whose Spinozistic view of nature and disillusionment with humanity results in an inordinate fondness for animals. F. S. Dry, who first pointed out this 'source',[5] has noted that there is also a curious parallel, in the 'Mucklestane' of this story, the 'huge column of unhewn granite' that dominates the setting, to the image Charlotte uses in her Preface for *Wuthering Heights*: 'The statuary found a granite block on a solitary moor . . .'

An Irish tale published in *Blackwood's* in November 1840, by Bartholomew Simmonds, is a stronger candidate, in that Emily Brontë consciously or unconsciously recalled it in more detail when writing *Wuthering Heights*. The Bridegroom of Barna certainly formed part of the literary experience fused into the novel.[6] (One feels that had Simmonds read *Wuthering Heights* he might have charged Emily Brontë with plagiarism.) Though in detail the plots differ, there is a broad resemblance in the elements of separated lovers and outcast hero. Hugh Lawlor's love for Ellen Nugent is frustrated, not by a socially better match, but because he is wanted for murder immediately after their marriage. Ellen becomes another frenzied heroine dying of shock after her lover's brief return; it is a death imaginatively very inferior to that of Catherine. There is an extravagant scene in which Lawlor is captured while embracing her exhumed body; it is like Heathcliff's account of how he broke into Catherine's grave. The colouring of the two heroines whose appearance has a common ancestry in Scott's novels is not, of course, proof of influence. (Harriet Martineau stated that Charlotte told her sisters they were wrong, even morally wrong, to make their heroines beautiful as a matter of course.[7])

Ellen Nugent, in *The Bridegroom of Barna*, is 'one of the brightest and most delicate creatures I ever beheld. Her pale gold hair, deep blue, melancholy eyes and pale, colourless cheek combined with a form light and faerylike as ever danced in a moonbeam, remind one less of an earthly being than of some mournful angel doomed for a while to hover among mankind.'[8] 'A wild, wick slip' Catherine was, according to Mrs Dean, 'but she had the bonniest eye, and sweetest smile, and lightest foot in the parish' (ch. v). The latter attribute may have originated in the hero, who is thus addressed by the somewhat Nelly-Dean-like fortune-teller, Nanse: 'Yerrah, Master Hugh, I wouldn't doubt your step to be the nimblest in the room . . . you had ever the swiftest foot in the barony.'[9] Nanse has a choric role and also acts as go-between for the lovers. The closest parallel between this rustic melodrama by an obscure writer and *Wuthering Heights* is the scene in which Lawlor returns to Ellen on a summer evening.

It was far in summer. At the close of a sweet evening in July
Ellen sat alone in the window of her chamber that opened on the
deep, soft grass and refreshing umbrage of the orchard by which
the greater part of the mansion was overshadowed. The air was
sweet with the fragrance of lime trees, and slumberous with the
lulling hum of bees. . . . she raised her eyes to the brightening
stars. When she dropped them again, Lawlor was standing close
to her, his very breath almost mingling with the rich shadows
of her hair.[10]

'When she dropped them' – such penny-a-line writing shows what
Emily Brontë made of the romance, but (with a slight change of
season) this passage is paralleled very closely by that describing
Heathcliff's first appearance, after his long absence, to Nelly
Dean.

On a mellow evening in September I was coming from the garden with a heavy basket of apples which I had been gathering.
It had got dusk, and the moon looked over the high wall of the
court, causing undefined shadows to lurk in the corners of the
numerous projecting portions of the building. I set my burden
on the house steps by the kitchen door, and lingered to rest,
and drew in a few more breaths of the soft, sweet air; my eyes
were on the moon, and my back to the entrance, when I heard
a voice behind me say –
    'Nelly, is that you?' (ch. x)

'That must indeed be a depraved mind which can gather evil
from . . . *Macbeth* and *Hamlet* and *Julius Caesar*', Charlotte Brontë
commented in her 1834[11] reading list. The Shakespearean
quality of *Wuthering Heights* was claimed by the earliest critics, such
as G. W. Peck, writing in the *American Review* in June 1848.
Bonamy Dobrée has compared the book to the *Oresteia* or *King
Lear*.[12] To encounter English romantic literature is generally to
be conscious of the influence of Shakespeare, but *Wuthering
Heights* is more indebted to Shakespeare than perhaps any
other English novel. Most obviously indebted in its dramatic
intensity and its secondary use of such dateless motivations as
revenge and avarice. ('Legitimate Edgar, I must have your land

. . .'¹³) Fiction is not a performing art, and one must concede that for the most distinctive and novelistic qualities of *Wuthering Heights*, models – Shakespearean or otherwise – were not available.

In addition to a certain presiding spirit in *Wuthering Heights*, the fact that King Lear and Milo are (I believe) the only characters in art mentioned in the text, and an Elizabethan extravagance, there is an actual Shakespearean residue which suggests that Emily Brontë underwent the experience of the tragedies with unusual force. For instance, in the sadistic scenes in which the younger Catherine is confined at Wuthering Heights and Heathcliff is destroying Linton, his son, the dialogue has a very Jacobean quality, intense, yet bantering and colloquial.

Come, come – have done and get to bed. In a month or two, my lad, you'll be able to pay her back her present tyrannies with a vigorous hand. You're pining for pure love, are you not? nothing else in the world; and she shall have you! There, to bed! Zillah won't be here tonight; you must undress yourself. Hush! hold your noise! Once in your own room, I'll not come near you, you needn't fear. (ch. XXVII)

It is Websterian, and may have a darker meaning for those who subscribe to the theory that Catherine is Heathcliff's daughter. But it is surely based, consciously or otherwise, on Othello's 'Get you to bed on the instant . . . dismiss your attendant there . . .' Both the atmosphere of pending destruction and the detail, the dismissal of the servant, paralleled by Zillah's absence, are the same. *Wuthering Heights* is not a silver-fork novel, in which the children are undressed by their maids. (On the other hand, this detail is well prepared for by Zillah's derelictions already described.)

The movement of the passage, and the thick-coming succession of spoken clauses are evidence of the force and coherence of its creator's imagination. On such evidence there is something in the suggestion that a potential dramatist was lost in Emily Brontë's early death. She is most impressive when this sombre side is uppermost.

Then there is Joseph's description, as reported by Isabella, of the roistering that enables Heathcliff to win Hindley Earnshaw's property (ch. x). 'This is the way on't – up at sun dahn; dice, brandy, cloised shutters, and can'le lught till next day, at nooin.' Leaving out of account the reality of the dialect – it is like nothing spoken anywhere – it echoes both the substance and the sequence of *King Lear*, in portions of Acts III and IV:

> we'll go to supper in the morning; so, so, so.
> And I'll go to bed at noon.

Gloster later says: 'Knows't thou the way to Dover?' and Edgar replies, 'Both stile and gate, horse way and foot-path.' Joseph in *Wuthering Heights* continues his 'speech': 'her father's son gallops dahn t' broad road, while he flees afore to oppen t'pikes'. It is perhaps coincidence that the dialogue in *Lear* is between father and son (Gloster and Edgar). The action of the play becomes the metaphor of the novel. Joseph, cackling and moralising, is a kind of Fool. Other parallels between the tragedies and *Wuthering Heights* have been pointed out. *Wuthering Heights* is no Elizabethan pastiche, like *The Cenci*, or *Otho the Great*; rather, Shakespeare guided Emily Brontë's hand at certain moments of figurative expression. The romantic resolution of the tragedy in *Wuthering Heights* by means of the younger generation owes something to the late plays. For instance, the 'disclosure' of Catherine and Hareton during Lockwood's last visit seems to show a more than accidental resemblance to the end of *The Tempest*. In at least hinting at the possibility of a brave new world at the end of *Wuthering Heights*, Emily Brontë acknowledged a debt.

Ever since Émile Montégut, reviewing *The Life of Charlotte Brontë* in *La Revue des Deux Mondes* in 1857, called Emily 'petite sœur d'Hoffmann'[14] the suggestion (not uncontested) has recurred that *Wuthering Heights* owes something to Hoffmann, and particularly to *Das Majorat* (*The Entail*). In her introduction to *Wuthering Heights* Mrs Humphry Ward went so far as to state that it represents the grafting of a European – and specifically German – tradition upon a mind already richly stored with English and local reality.[15] As I have said earlier there is evidence, from

Brussels and from Mrs Gaskell via Ellen Nussey, that Emily
Brontë knew some German, but of what she read or how proficient
she was in the language nothing is known, unless we are to take as
evidence a quotation from Schiller on the lips of a fictional
character resembling her. Certainly German had the esoteric
attraction for intelligent Victorian women that Russian has for
their descendants. The innate Puritanism, seriousness and feeling
for nature of *Wuthering Heights* could be claimed to be characteristic
of the English imagination: on the other hand its symmetry and
schematisation, its technical sophistication and treatment of a
romantic attachment as a sacred and fatal mission are characteristic
of more 'serious' German fiction than Hoffmann's. Such, for
instance, as Goethe's novels (*Kindred by Choice* and *Wilhelm
Meister*), which were discussed in *Blackwood's Magazine*[16] during
Emily's lifetime, and later by G. H. Lewes. *The Entail* is, of
course, fundamentally unlike *Wuthering Heights*, but there are a
number of detail resemblances from which it is tempting to
conclude that Emily Brontë had read it. Nor, I think, was it the
only tale by Hoffmann she was at least indirectly familiar with.
She need not have read them in the original, in fact one might
think that the indications are otherwise. One clue is that a selection of German tales, including *Das Majorat* and works by de la
Motte Fouqué, Pichler and Kreuse, translated by the Edinburgh
scholar and friend of De Quincey, R. P. Gillies, was published by
Blackwood and Cadell in 1826. It was reviewed (by De Quincey)
in *Blackwood's Magazine* in December 1826.

The typically complex plot of *The Entail* concerns fratricide
and dispossession and their effects on the lives of three generations
of Baltic noblemen. Hoffmann was writing about country that he
knew, and the story is less Hoffmannesque than many of the
tales, combining realism with the mysterious in what has become
a standard mode of the thriller. The opening (the section most
often related to *Wuthering Heights*) describes the narrator, assistant
to the family lawyer on temporary business at the castle of
Rolandsitten, retiring for the night with a copy of Schiller's
Ghost-Seer, to be woken by the usual gloomy old servant re-
enacting his part in the murder. The gaps are subsequently filled

in by the lawyer in a series of narrative flash-backs. Like most of
the tales it is much too complex, producing the usual sensations of
déjà vu when, for instance, the collapse of the first baron's observa-
tory is followed by that of the audience-chamber. Hoffmann's
effects work like the cinema of Resnais and Robbe-Grillet,
creating a dream-like atmosphere of apparent confusion (as the
Blackwood's reviewer of another translated tale, *The Devil's Elixir*,
noted[17]). A light and realistic flirtation between the baroness and
the young man is inserted into the mystery story.

This Baltic castle is no place of moral teething, merely one of
winter-sports. But other details, apart from the ghostly scratching
of the opening, suggest a relationship to a reader familiar with
Wuthering Heights; for instance the final abandonment of the
stormily situated castle for a more sheltered site, a change which
is pointed out to the narrator on his last visit. Another haunted
castle of romanticism in one of the most terrifying and complex
of Hoffmann's stories, *The Devil's Elixir*, may be more closely
related to the opening of *Wuthering Heights*. This is the lodge of the
forest ranger where the monk Medardus takes refuge during his
tortuous wanderings and encounters with his *Doppelgänger*. The
interior of Wuthering Heights is a regional variant of this realistic
German lodge and (announced by an old servant, 'Christian')
Medardus's first encounter with the *Oberrevier-förster* is strikingly
similar to Lockwood's with Heathcliff. The ways of life centred
on the houses have something in common, and both are places of
salutary ordeal for their visitors. 'To such people every situation in
the country appears both lonely and stupid', says the *Förster*, 'but
much depends on the temper and disposition of the party by
whom a house like this is inhabited.' The details of the subsequent
nightmare in which Medardus encounters and grapples with his
Doppelgänger only to wake and find it true seem to me much closer
to Lockwood's experience with Catherine's ghost than anything in
The Entail.

The Devil's Elixir was published in English in 1824, and a
review by Lockhart and Gillies (from which the above quotation,
part of a longer extract, is taken) appeared in *Blackwood's* in July
that year. Here, perhaps, is another instance of the influence on

Emily Brontë of material quoted in the periodicals. She was, of course, only six when this issue appeared, but there is other evidence of the Brontës' familiarity with *Blackwood's* at this period. (Even so, such a persistent early memory, if that is what it was, is surprising.) The diction of this translation is similar to that of *Wuthering Heights*: 'a reaming flagon of home-brewed ale, with another of Stettiner beer . . .' and 'she did not stay to retaliate, but re-entered in a minute, bearing a reaming silver pint . . .' (ch. XXXII). 'Reaming' or frothing, is Scots, but also occurs in Yorkshire, a fact that does not clarify the issue of whether there was a merger between the Gimmerton and Stettin breweries.

The plot of *Wuthering Heights* in the ordinary sense, that of a passionate attachment frustrated by a socially more convenient match, is evidently of a type common at the time, perhaps because of awareness of social conditions. It is found in *Maud*, in *Aylmer's Field* and in *Locksley Hall*. It is also archetypal. Similarities to fairy-story or folk-tale have been pointed out in *Wuthering Heights*, such as the ritual feeding and dressing of Catherine when she enters the new world of the Lintons on her first visit to the Grange. Emily Brontë's imagination was evidently attracted by the dramatic simplicity and vivid quality of the ballads, but this primitive unsophisticated strength was already available in her own existence, and that of her family, which has become legendary. (Her treatment of romance has been influential, to judge from a popular modern novel such as L. P. Hartley's *The Go-Between*.) She was very probably influenced by an example of the Tennysonian 'youthful attachment betrayed' theme in the life of Byron. The connection is perhaps not directly with his poem 'The Dream',[18] but with the incident on which it was based as told by Moore. The story is, even now, a compelling one. It is not difficult to see it becoming part of the private mythology of Emily Brontë, with her response to enduring emotion.

It was in the year 1803 that his [Byron's] heart, already twice as we have seen possessed with the childish notion that it loved, conceived an attachment which, young as he was, even then for such a feeling – sunk so deep into his mind as to give a colour to all his future life. That unsuccessful loves are generally the most lasting is a truth, however sad, which unluckily does not require this instance to confirm it. To the same cause, I fear, must be traced the perfect innocence and romance which distinguish this early attachment to Miss Chaworth from the many others that succeeded it, without effacing it in his heart; – making it the only one whose details can be entered into with safety or whose results, however darkening their influence on himself, can be dwelt upon with pleasurable interest by others ...

... To the family of Miss Chaworth, who resided at Annesley, in the immediate neighbourhood of Newstead, he had been made known some time before, in London, and now renewed his acquaintanceship with them. The young heiress herself combined many worldly advantages that encircled her, much personal beauty, and a disposition the most amiable and attaching. Though already fully alive to her charms, it was at the period of which we speak that the young poet, who was then in his sixteenth year, while the object of his admiration was about two years older, seems to have drunk deepest of that fascination whose effects were to be so lasting; – six short summer weeks which he passed in her company being sufficient to lay the foundation of a feeling for all life.

He used at first, though offered a bed at Annesley, to return every night to sleep, alleging as a reason that he was afraid of the family pictures of the Chaworths, that he fancied 'they had taken a grudge to him on account of the duel, and would come down from their frames at night to haunt him.' At length one evening, he said gravely to Miss Chaworth and her cousin: 'In going home last night I saw a *bogle*'; which Scotch term being wholly unintelligible to the young ladies, he explained that he had seen a ghost, and would not therefore return to Newstead that evening. . . . In the dances in the evening at Matlock, Miss Chaworth of course joined, while her lover sat looking on, solitary and mortified. It is not impossible, indeed, that the dislike which he always expressed for this amusement may have originated in some bitter pang felt in his youth, on seeing 'the lady of his love' led out by others, to the gay dance to which he was himself excluded.[19]

The elements in this passage – the emotion colouring an entire life, the family portraits, the supernatural, the social exclusion of the hero – related to *Wuthering Heights*, need no stressing. But the incident showing the most striking parallel is described by Moore as follows:

Miss Chaworth looked on Byron as a mere schoolboy. He was in his manners, too, at that period, rough and odd, and (as I have heard from more than one quarter) by no means popular among girls of his own age. If at any moment, however, he had flattered himself with the hope of being loved by her, a circumstance mentioned in his Memoranda as one of the most painful of those humiliations to which the defect in his foot had exposed him, must have let the truth in with dreadful certainty upon his heart. He either was told of, or overheard, Miss Chaworth saying to her maid, 'Do you think I could care for that lame boy?' This speech, as he himself described it, was like a shot through the heart. Though late at night when he heard it, he instantly darted out of the house and scarcely knowing whither he ran, never stopped till he found himself at Newstead.[20]

Heathcliff overhears Catherine telling Mrs Dean that it would degrade her to marry him (ch. IX) and runs away. The situations are not, of course, identical in all respects, but the resemblance is remarkable. With the other parallels it indicates that Heathcliff is not only 'Byronic', he is also, in part, modelled, consciously or unconsciously, on Byron himself. (In 1805, relates Moore, Miss Chaworth married Mr John Musters, and the news was received by Byron with Heathcliffian stoicism.)

It is worth mentioning that Byron's life influenced the Gondal prototypes of the characters of *Wuthering Heights*. Moore quotes some then-unpublished verses by Byron, a lament for Mary Chaworth:

> Hills of Annesley, bleak and barren
> Where my thoughtless childhood strayed
> How the northern tempests warring
> Howl above thy tufted shade!
> Now no more the hour beguiling,
> Former favourite haunts I see;
> Now no more my Mary smiling,
> Makes ye seem a heaven to me.[21]

Characteristically Emily Brontë created from this two contrasting 'songs', 'By Julius Brenzaida to G.S.' (H80 and 81), both dated 17 October 1838. Evidently the Gondal characters enacted Byron's loss long before the novel was written. Moore also quotes some lines pencilled by Byron in a 'volume of Mme de Maintenon's Letters', stating in a footnote that they are by Lady Tute and published in 1796.

> Oh Memory, torture me no more
> The present's all o'ercast . . .
>
> Past pleasure doubles present pain
> To sorrow adds regret,
> Regret and hope are both in vain
> I ask, but to – forget.[22]

This is echoed in Emily Brontë's 'The wind, I hear it sighing' (H120):

> Yet could I with past pleasures
> Past woe's oblivion buy,
> That by the death of my dearest treasures
> My deadliest pains might die . . .

There are other indications in Emily Brontë's poems that Byron's life, 'the 'wildering maze/Of mad hours left behind' (H142) was the model for the Gondal characters.

Byron's 'The Dream', a fine poem in his intense but non-strident manner (that of the 'Lines on hearing that Lady Byron was Ill', composed about the same period), contains the substance of the same incident in concentrated form. It has elements not occurring in Moore, which also parallel those of *Wuthering Heights*, such as the Byron-figure's disappearance abroad.

> The Boy was sprung to manhood: in the wilds
> Of fiery climes he made himself a home,
> And his soul drank their sunbeams: he was girt
> With strange and dusky aspects; he was not
> Himself like what he had been; on the sea
> And on the shore he was a wanderer: . . .

The Chaworth-figure, 'the lady of his love', marries and is happily circumstanced, but, like Catherine Earnshaw, declines into frenzied melancholia.

> her mind
> Had wander'd from its dwelling, and her eyes
> They had not their own lustre, but the look
> Which is not of the earth; she was become
> The queen of a fantastic realm; her thoughts
> Were combinations of disjointed things;
> And forms impalpable and unperceived
> Of others' sight familiar were to hers.
> And this the world calls frenzy; but the wise
> Have a far deeper madness, and the glance
> Of melancholy is a fearful gift;
> What is it but the telescope of truth?

The Boy becomes The Wanderer, like Byron, a romantic outcast and artist-figure. The poem ends with a summary.

> It was of a strange order, that the doom
> Of these two creatures should be thus traced out
> Almost like a reality – the one
> To end in madness – both in misery.

Evidently, to consider Byron's life and work in relation to Emily Brontë is to enter a hall of mirrors. But they are not plane mirrors.

A year after Emily's death, Charlotte told her publisher that she would like to read William Godwin's *Caleb Williams*.[23] There is no evidence that her sister had been familiar with it – or that she had not. But there are common features in Godwin's masterpiece and in *Wuthering Heights*, which make the possible connection of interest: elements such as predetermined design and the character of the hero. Caleb Williams, Falkland his master and Heathcliff share as romantic outcasts fierce energy and predestinating obsessions. In *Caleb Williams* (revived during the current fashion for the Gothic novel) Godwin combined such characteristics with those of the *roman à thèse*. In this instance there are the themes of the class struggle and social betterment, also embodied in the conception of Heathcliff and in the dialectic narrative form of *Wuthering Heights*, in which the torch of improvement is handed on to Hareton.[24]

Some ideas in *Caleb Williams*, such as the all-sufficiency of the imagination as a support in adversity (exemplified in the prison scenes), would have had a special appeal to the prisoner Brontës. There is a striking similarity, which could be due to common sources, in the mysticism expressed by the philosophic Mr Clare in Godwin's novel and in that of Heathcliff.

> Falkland, said he, after having appeared for a short time absorbed in thought, I feel that I am dying. This is a strange distemper of mine . . . (*Caleb Williams*, ch. v)

> Nelly [remarks Heathcliff] there is a strange change approaching; I'm in its shadow at present. I take so little interest in my daily life that I hardly remember to eat or drink . . . (ch. xxxiii)

Mr Clare continues:

> It is vain that I muster all my spirits to my heart. The enemy is too mighty and too merciless for me; he will not give me time so much as to breathe. These things are not yet in our power; they are parts of a great series that is perpetually flowing. (*Caleb Williams*, ch. v)

And Heathcliff:

> And yet I cannot continue in this condition! I have to remind myself to breathe – almost to remind my heart to beat! And it is like bending back a stiff spring: it is by compulsion that I do the slightest act not prompted by one thought, and by compulsion that I notice anything, alive or dead, which is not associated with one universal idea. (ch. xxxiii)

Emily Brontë's probable response to such ideas as Mr Clare's needs no stressing. In *Caleb Williams* he proceeds to the theme of human improvement: in *Wuthering Heights* the stress is on the transcendental nature of love. Emily does not share Godwin's optimism; she has looked into her heart and found the same corruption there. She may, however, have been interested in his narrative methods, as outlined in the Preface to *Caleb Williams*. *Wuthering Heights* is so constructed that it can have been written only in a way similar to that described so graphically by Godwin, that is, with the end implicit in the beginning. 'The unity of interest and spirit in a tale truly considered', he wrote, 'gives it a powerful hold on the reader which can scarcely be generated with equal success in any other way.'

Caleb Williams seems not to have been known at Haworth parsonage, from Charlotte's remark quoted above, at any rate to her. It was, however, appearing in cheap editions, such as Bentley's series of popular novels, in the 1830s.

If the parallels suggested above are the result of actual conscious or unconscious influence, then more books than one would guess indeed contributed to *Wuthering Heights*: Scott, popular magazine fiction, Hoffmann, Shakespeare, Godwin, Moore and periodical reviewing. If Emily's models helped her to write a work acceptable to the book market of the 1840s, her outdoing of some of her sources in truth and power went some way to alienate it. The text of *Wuthering Heights*, one may think, indicates that much in what Janet Spens called the 'plurality of latent experience'[25] in her work is literary. An unpremeditated novelist – if this was the case – and limited in experience, her mind was nourished by literature much as that of most novelists is nourished by observation. Literary relatives of her characters are certainly easier to find than human originals.

In these respects *Wuthering Heights* is alone among novels, in being an original work containing materials pre-existing in literature. Emily Brontë's sources were sometimes embodied piecemeal, virtually in paraphrase, in her text. This recall of art is characteristic of the Brontë imagination and situation; it is manifest in their early writings and, for instance, in Charlotte's recollection of paintings and illustrations in her novels.[26] The force of *Wuthering Heights*, one may feel, derives partly from its concentration of powerful literary elements. The novel as form, however, is pre-eminently concerned with original experience of life, and opinions may differ as to how this aspect affects Emily Brontë's total achievement. Those who think *Wuthering Heights* is in some ways a freakish, claustrophobic work may here find support. On the other hand its undoubted power and originality may seem a triumph of the imagination over unpropitious circumstances. But it is time to consider the work not as derivative, but as itself.

3. *Wuthering Heights* now

SOME necessary judgements and distinctions are now familiar and accepted: *Wuthering Heights* is a great novel, a classic in its enduring interest and wide popularity. Its success in this latter respect calls to mind G. H. Lewes's tribute to the drawing power of *Hamlet*: 'Only consider what striking effects it has.'[1] There is no need to repeat the case for its essential difference and artistic superiority compared with the historical romances, Gothic tales or Godwinian novels of ideas which it can be compared to, in certain respects, and which may have influenced it.

It is also, I think, accepted (at any rate in most reasonable quarters) that although as a 'regional' novel the book reflects to some degree a particular society and period, it is realistic in such a way that some of the usual approaches, such as consideration of its truth to the operation of character in society (the themes of Jane Austen or George Eliot), are closed, or partly closed. 'Completely removed from the stir of society', remarks Lockwood, on entering that country, and he concludes like Prospero. ' "Gimmerton" I repeated – my residence in that locality had already grown dim and dreamy' (ch. XXXII).

'Prose fiction' is here a more useful term than 'novel', for the news is about figures that seem to belong to ballad or legend, and the presence of living narrators reinforces the impression. John Wain suggests[2] that in eighteenth-century Yorkshire people could cultivate their obsessions in lonely places, so that the book also 'stands up' as realistic narrative. But it stands up without this information, and indeed our sense of region is the Brontës' doing to a great extent. Nor, I think, can *Wuthering Heights* be reasonably interpreted as some kind of allegorical or symbolic statement about the nascent power of the proletariat, though Emily Brontë's poems and the dominant questions of her age support the idea that some awareness of the dynamic of common humanity, some liberal consciousness, contributed to the creation of Heathcliff and Hareton.

Lockwood's hints do not indicate that *Wuthering Heights* is unrealistic, for no novel can be that. They imply a bias towards the extreme, the exceptional. These qualities are not necessarily incompatible with the novel of social or documentary significance, but the most useful interpretations of *Wuthering Heights* have shown it as, first and foremost (as far as the totality of a work of fiction can have an abstract 'meaning'), 'about' states of mind and of nature, of man in the widest sense, not states of society. The inevitable question of what these states may be, their interest and relation to life and experience, is not an easy one to answer; it is connected not only with what the book says – or what characters in it may say – but is also inseparable from what it is, how it is made. One cannot help noticing that studies of particular, subsidiary aspects of *Wuthering Heights* have provided more acceptable answers than attempts to pin down this meaning. Is the book to be understood as a tragic romance of noble natures destroyed by circumstances, or as some kind of allegory about the play of psychological and natural forces, the workings of life in the most general sense? Neither view seems quite to take account of the whole experience. Is *Wuthering Heights* the perfect work of art that it has been claimed to be, or have important reservations to be made? To what extent is it a realisation of its author's intentions, or a process of involuntary self-discovery? Recent criticism has been devoted to this problem of maturity.

The plot of *Wuthering Heights* (in the baldest sense a traditional situation of romance), the development of a passionate relationship between the foundling Heathcliff and Catherine Earnshaw, its betrayal by her and the consequences, is communicated to the reader in a complicated and sophisticated way – itself part of the statement – by means of two narrators. The story is introduced at a point near its conclusion by the outer narrator, Lockwood, who is brought up to date by the inner one, Nelly Dean, before temporarily leaving the scene. He returns to hear the conclusion and to experience for himself the concluding state of the novel's world.

Around the focal situation is organised a whole system of contrasts and correspondences manifest in the other characters and in nature. The schematic arrangement of *Wuthering Heights*, first clearly demonstrated by David Cecil,[3] includes the contrast between the 'stormy' and 'calm' families: morally and psychologically Heathcliff and the Earnshaws on one side, and the Lintons on the other, are to different scales, with differing demands from life. These hereditary characteristics are further emphasised by the setting and atmosphere of the two houses. The families have each a single son and daughter, and the last of each line are joined at the end.

Elaborate presentation is certainly one characteristic *Wuthering Heights* shares with Gothic fiction (for instance, *Melmoth the Wanderer*, *The Confessions of a Justified Sinner* or innumerable mystery stories before and since which are related by means of journals, letters, memoranda, etc.). But Emily Brontë's method is integral and essential to the work in a way that implies a quite different order of art. The story commences with a date, and is, in its entirety, Lockwood's journal, comprising his experience in the 'present' and Mrs Dean's in the past. Can such a perennial artistic objection as the charge that this is a confusing or unsuccessful method of telling a story be quite without foundation? Emily Brontë certainly got her folds right, and this control is part of the aesthetic experience of the book. Whether the reader looking for relaxation finds it a lucid and engaging method is another matter. *Wuthering Heights* stretches the attention of the examining (if not the immediately experiencing) mind to the utmost, over octaves of reported events.

Both Mrs Dean's voice and Lockwood's pen are essential to the meaning of the book. Besides carrying the conviction of eye-witness accounts, so important when extraordinary events are being related, each provides its own assessment and judgement of the values involved, its own particular irony. Ellen's matter-of-fact voice sounds only within the confines of the story; Lockwood's is a link with the outside world. He represents partly the artificiality of the 'stirring society' of town. His values contrast with the particular pastoral, not exactly summed up by terms such as 'rustic', 'simple' or 'romantic', of *Wuthering Heights* itself. There is a subsidiary emphasis on a form of quietism related to the disciplines of contemplation, and of creation.

> 'Are you acquainted with the mood of mind in which, if you were seated alone, and the cat licking its kitten on the rug before you, you would watch the operation so intently that puss's neglect of one ear would put you seriously out of temper?'
> 'A terribly lazy mood, I should say.'
> 'On the contrary, a tiresomely active one. It is mine at present, and therefore continue minutely. I perceive that people in these regions acquire over people in towns the value that a spider in a dungeon does over a spider in a cottage, to their various occupants; and yet the deepened attraction is not entirely owing to the situation of the looker-on. They do live more in earnest, more in themselves, and less in surface change and frivolous external things. I could fancy a love for life here almost possible.' (ch. VII)

It is not entirely unequivocal, that dungeon suggests a murmur of revolt, but the values ostensibly advocated are those of such a Romantic manifesto as the Preface to *Lyrical Ballads*. Lockwood gets the chance of emotional commitment, and turns it down. His handling – and he must have been very difficult to handle – is extremely ingenious. There had to be a motive for bringing him north, so he is shown, not as the city slicker (seldom indecisive, like Lockwood), but as an intending misanthrope whose desire for solitude does not stand the test. He not only reports events as an outsider, but also provides an important historical dimension; he is mediator between past, present and future.

Nelly Dean is a more fully drawn, functional character (her age can be worked out, like that of most of the principal characters, from information casually dropped, or so it seems), and she plays a bigger part. The protagonists exist for most of their lives in her memory, the history to Lockwood's present time. She has read

'more books than you would guess', but her comments are not
necessarily for the reader to agree with. She is more than a
camera or the occupant of a checkpoint where the others report
events; her impartiality and innocence have been questioned; as
well as being 'judge, interpreter, chorus, attorney',[4] there is something about her of Pandarus.

The imputation of lack of self-awareness in Emily Brontë's presentation of passion in *Wuthering Heights* was first made by her
sister, and it has been repeated since by Cecil Day Lewis, for
example:

> Emily was a moralist on more than one level. We can accept it
> that she was unconscious of the full moral significance of
> *Wuthering Heights* – its lurid and uncompromising antinomian-
> ism, in which passion is substituted for grace, as the justification
> for an overriding of the moral law. It is difficult indeed to
> imagine how the creator of Heathcliff and Catherine could have
> consciously received the full charge of that moral electricity
> and lived.[5]

Such a charge against a carefully constructed work should be
made warily, and one might think that it is in the presentation of
the passion of the central situation that there is most evidence of
mind and of conscious control of the reader's response. The functions of the narrators can, I think, be connected with external
evidence in a way that strongly suggests her awareness of the
values presented. (The lack of self-awareness perhaps shows itself
in a slightly different way.) Whether there is wholehearted commitment to any set of values, any unequivocal substitution of
passion for grace is another question.

The celebrated opening of *Wuthering Heights* shows how Emily
Brontë could make absolutely integral use of such well-worn
properties as the visit of the stranger to a mysterious house and
the dream. Both of Lockwood's dreams are related to the work as
a whole, to its central situation and its themes. In the second and
more important of them, the 'mystic' spirit hand and the clutch-
ing hand of the Gothic tale are used with great imaginative power:
the intensity here is appropriate to the introduction to the central
situation it provides. Lockwood's prying into Catherine's journal

and decipherment of the writing on the window ledge establish her childhood attachment to Heathcliff, their rebellious natures, and her tragic choice (in the alternating names, Catherine Earnshaw – Catherine Heathcliff – Catherine Linton). His discoveries also provide the waking basis for the dream of her ghost, thus linking the planes of the real and the supernatural. 'An immediate interest kindled in me for the unknown Catherine.'

The first nightmare is presented in a more relaxed tone, but the Rev. Branderham's sermon on Matthew 18: 21–2 ('How oft shall my brother sin against me, and I forgive him?') has, perhaps, a recondite significance. E. F. Shannon has shown that this is the text on which the interminable discourse is delivered – it is not, of course, cited – and he suggests that the unforgivable sin is Catherine's infidelity.[6] Her defiance of God is another possibility. This dream is thus related both to Lockwood's discoveries and to the following dream; it also reflects, with true dream-logic, the uncomfortable evening preceding his retirement. (The attack on him when he attempts to escape from the house becomes the assault by Branderham's congregation.)

Wuthering Heights is a remarkably dramatised novel; there is no direct comment by the author and a minimum of reflection divorced from action as 'scene' follows 'scene' and the characters are hastened to their various fates. There is nothing like this in nineteenth-century literature until Ibsen. Comparisons with poetic drama are not misplaced. Nevertheless, the House of Fiction must retain a place for a tale so thoroughly told as this.

The main narrative structure has the function of communicating the central situation, Catherine's disloyalty to Heathcliff and its consequences, with maximum effect, and modulating from it to a tolerable norm of life. The story is impressive as tragic romance, but it may be useful to consider to what extent it is meaningfully romantic in the sense or senses in which the term is used in the history of ideas. The situation embodies a whole hierarchy of emotions and attitudes. Some are manifest in Catherine's exchanges with Mrs Dean before her marriage. She explains that she has pledged herself to Linton, and seeks reassurance. Her reasons for her decision are social in the more superficial

and conventional sense. Throughout, Mrs Dean plays her choric
role as Catherine's conscience. She not only posits more austere
values, but hints at the largely fortuitous aspect of social relationships.

> 'I'm very far from jesting, Miss Catherine,' I replied. 'You
> love Mr Edgar because he is handsome, and young, and cheerful,
> and rich, and loves you. That last, however, goes for nothing –
> You would love him without that, probably, and with it, you
> wouldn't, unless he possessed the four former attractions.'
> 'No, to be sure not – I should only pity him – hate him,
> perhaps, if he were ugly, and a clown.'
> 'But there are several other handsome, rich young men in the
> world; handsomer, possibly, than he and richer – what should
> hinder you from loving them?'
> 'If there be any, they are out of my way – I've seen none like
> Edgar.'
> 'You may see some; and he won't always be handsome, and
> young, and may not always be rich.'
> 'He is now, and I have only to do with the present – I wish
> you would speak rationally.' (ch. ix)

The moralist shows here, preparing, with her 'I have only to
do with the present', for Catherine's subsequent and celebrated
statement of her position. (Even the most convenient of marriages
is not usually on quite such a superficial basis.) But one notes the
clear-sightedness – 'what should hinder you from loving them' of
the 'passionate' novelist. In an otherwise admirable essay,[7] Derek
Traversi's reading of Mrs Dean's attitude ('Nelly . . . maintains
that Edgar is a good match') is unfair to her; Nelly does nothing
of the kind.

The complicated nature of the situation is very evident in what
follows, Catherine's fuller account of her feelings and of her celebrated dream, already referred to in connection with the poem
'The Philosopher'.

> It would degrade me to marry Heathcliff now; so he shall never
> know how I love him; and that, not because he's handsome,
> Nelly, but because he's more myself than I am. Whatever our
> souls are made of, his and mine are the same, and Linton's is as

different as a moonbeam from lightning, or frost from fire. (ch. IX)

Apart from the reference to souls, no values are referred to. Mere identity of substance is neutral. 'Whatever our souls are made of . . .' Yet 'I've no more business to marry Edgar Linton than I have to be in heaven'. One can only wonder what this affinity is, that denies a right to heaven, especially when there follows an explicit connection with the enduring and the transcendental.

I cannot express it; but surely you and everybody have a notion that there is or should be an existence of yours beyond you. What were the use of my creation if I were entirely contained here? . . . My love for Linton is like the foliage in the woods: time will change it, I'm well aware, as winter changes the trees. My love for Heathcliff resembles the eternal rocks beneath – a source of little visible delight, but necessary. Nelly, I *am* Heathcliff –

Of course, this works satisfactorily as a lyrical statement of romantic love, with the weight of the well-realised childhoods of Heathcliff and Catherine behind it: their love is associated with daring and hardihood and independence. (We have already experienced the contrast with the Lintons, when the pair look in through the window of the Grange at the young Isabella and Edgar quarrelling over a lapdog.)

The chapters describing Heathcliff's return, as the 'person from Gimmerton', and the two triangular encounters involving the lovers and – briefly in the second of them – Edgar are crucial. Between them is an episode providing a measure of contrast, that of Isabella's elopement (vital to the action of the remainder of the novel). It says much for Emily Brontë's power of making all disagreeables evaporate that the fact that Heathcliff and Isabella are actually married before the last encounter goes almost unnoticed. Catherine's sickness and delirium follows the first meeting, and her death the second. It is worth asking the question 'Why does Catherine die?' which may seem as absurd as 'Why does Hamlet hesitate?' Because tragic heroines do? Catherine's motive-seeking is hardly convincing in terms of reality, and Emily Brontë herself hardly sounds convinced by it. It follows the first violent encounter between the two men.

> You are aware that I am in no way blameable in this matter. What possessed him to turn listener? Heathcliff's talk was outrageous, after you left us; but I could soon have diverted him from Isabella, and the rest meant nothing. Now, all is dashed by the fool's craving to hear evil of self that haunts some people like a demon! Had Edgar never gathered our conversation, he would never have been the worse for it. Really, when he opened on me in that unreasonable tone of displeasure after I had scolded Heathcliff till I was hoarse for *him*; I did not care, hardly, what they did to each other, especially as I felt that, however the scene closed, we should all be driven asunder for nobody knows how long! Well, if I cannot keep Heathcliff for my friend – if Edgar will be mean and jealous, I'll try to break their hearts by breaking my own. (ch. XI)

The motivation of *Wuthering Heights* in such a passage is somewhat awkward, and is not in harmony with the inner action, which seems to involve the author more deeply and impresses itself on the reader.

Wuthering Heights expresses a spectrum of themes, intended and perhaps unintended (though not necessarily less important or artistically effective), all of which form part of the experience of the book. One can take a structuralist approach.

> *Wuthering Heights* [Dorothy Van Ghent has written] exists for the mind as a tension between two kinds of reality, a restrictive reality of civilised manners and codes, and the anonymous unregenerate reality of natural energies. The poetic structure is a structure of variations on the possibility of breakthrough from one mode of being to the other.[8]

This is some way valid, but the dichotomy does not quite square with the fact that our sympathies are wholly on the side of the unregenerate in this culture-myth. One is tempted to ask: 'exists for whose mind?' The 'civilised manners and codes' represented – I take it – largely by the Lintons, involve 'natural energies', a bulldog, loosed by the weak on the two inquisitive children; pride of office ('to beard a magistrate in his den', says Edgar, pompously); petty cruelty, cowardice and selfishness. While the anonymous, unregenerate reality involves courage, sympathy, imagination, strength – qualities not unconnected with civilisation. The approach by structure or texture must largely ignore the consciousness of Catherine Earnshaw, and it seems to me that the traditional concept of 'character' and the individual utterances expressing it should not be neglected; though an exclusively face-value approach is likely to be equally limiting and misleading.

'Self-fulfilment' suggests itself as a central theme, but any novel is in a sense concerned with self-fulfilment (the author's, at least); the question of the kind of fulfilment and of its general relevance remains. It is also necessary to consider how the role of Heathcliff affects such a view.

To consider, first, one theme in terms of romanticism: Catherine's exchanges with Nelly before her marriage have revealed the extent and depth of the feelings Heathcliff arouses; they are what she lives by. (He is not an adequate object for them all, it has been said.[9]) Her concern with the transcendent is of a very nineteenth-century variety, in which individual immortality is associated with fulfilment in personal relationships, and is qualified-for by a superior emotional life on earth. The idea of such a relationship as a transcendental token is characteristic of a scientific age, which could not forget an age of faith, and occurs in that other Victorian tragedy, 'In Memoriam'.

> My love involves the love before;
> My love is vaster passion now;
> Tho' mixed with God and Nature thou,
> I seem to love thee more and more.

Such love is also a burden. Catherine and Heathcliff are members of an *élite* of the emotions; what they represent is symbolised by their setting: a grange is for hoarding. *Lockwood* has remarked that time stagnates at Wuthering Heights; but fires and pewter shine more brightly there than at the Grange. 'The glance/Of melancholy is a fearful gift'[10] – Catherine's madness is an extension of vision:

to Nelly she is 'morbid', but she has access to worlds denied to
her phlegmatic household (she arouses similar sympathy to that
felt for Emma Bovary); access to the death-presaging *Doppelgänger*
or 'fetch' in the mirror, to the fairy cave, to the pathetic memory
of the barren nest, and to the lost paradise of childhood. According to Emily Brontë's ideal vision of human relationships – already
expressed in the poems – Catherine's divided loyalties are
sufficient to kill her. G. D. Klingopulos's reading of the novel
comes near this view.

> The author appears to say – 'That is one kind of person. They
> live long, more contentedly, accepting and giving affection
> freely. But these others are also possible, and necessary, to whom
> common standards hardly apply. To these life is not a sub-
> mission to time, a round of gentleness and enjoyment and love.
> They were born to live more keenly, to suffer the claims of feel-
> ing more keenly, and to die young. They were neither wise nor
> good, but selfish, wilful and violent. They were not content.'[11]

There is some slight external evidence that Emily Brontë intended that the function of Lockwood should at least leave the
way open for such an interpretation. He hears the story, and he is
Nelly Dean's *patient*; his convalescence is juxtaposed with the
main narrative; as Catherine dies, he recovers. 'But never mind!'
he reflects. 'I'll extract wholesome medicine from Mrs Dean's
bitter herbs' (ch. XIV). In an article in *Fraser's Magazine*, June 1838,
there is an anticipation of his words. Is it a chance one? '. . . the
pious reader will find himself able to explain the apparent contradictions for himself, and out of its solution extract wholesome
though bitter medicine'. It occurs in an article on Shelley's
atheism, probably by J. A. Heraud.[12] (The Brontës took *Fraser's*
for an unknown period in the early 1830s.[13]) Lockwood's function
is to pose contradictions, as is that of Mrs Dean. Were Emily
Brontë's readers meant to take their medicine in the same way as
the uncommitted Lockwood? Is *he* an adequate standard by which
to condemn the lovers? I do not think that he makes the book a
moral tale in the simple way suggested by Richard Chase (though
a quotation does not do his essay justice). 'Lockwood is instructed
in the nature of a grand passion, but he and Emily Brontë

together are instructed in its final fruits, even roaring fires and a bed of ashes.'¹⁴

Lockwood provides an escape from the moral climate of the time; with his aid, Heathcliff and Catherine can seem to be judged more than they are. The tenuous link with Shelley is not needed to show that Emily Brontë's hypothesis may be of the same order as that of *Epipsychidion*. This view of *Wuthering Heights* as a work of high romantic protest, of the order of Keats's odes, is attractive. But, on the other hand, irony is a misleading term for the function of characters such as Lockwood, who are as useful for disguising or evading a point of view as for stating one. They can be either 'themselves' or the author, and it is not always clear which they are.

Other aspects of the book must be taken into account before granting it the status of fully achieved masterpiece of romantic protest. While recognising its power and perennial fascination, one must admit that they have troubled generations of readers. 'Who or what is Heathcliff?' David Daiches has asked, pertinently. 'You must e'en take it as a gift from God,' says Mr Earnshaw, but his view is not general. He has returned with the foundling(?) to Wuthering Heights. 'They entirely refused to have it in bed with them, or even in their rooms, and I had no more sense, so I put it on the landing of the stairs, hoping it might be gone on the morrow' (ch. IV). (The neuter pronoun was used of children in Victorian novels, so it is not necessarily dehumanising.) 'It', Dr Daiches had noted, is usually seen acting on others rather than in isolation. Heathcliff's behaviour also recalls popular apothegms about sex coming in at the window. Miss Van Ghent has pointed out the repetition of certain symbols or figures indicating exclusion: he is often seen at gates, windows and doorways. As she sees it, this motif is not confined to Heathcliff; various other examples will suggest themselves. The many exclusions or forced penetrations have a cumulative effect, they are part of the texture of the novel.

Heathcliff also has many attributes of the Satan-figure in literature and mythology, with his darkness, his sudden manifestations, his 'going to and fro in the world'. The younger

Catherine identifies him. 'You *are* miserable, are you not? Lonely,
like the devil and envious like him? Nobody loves you, nobody
will cry for you when you die!' (ch. XXIX). But he is certainly not
'the spirit that denies' or mere malevolence. If he is the devil, he
is a fallen angel and is described in terms that may owe something
to Milton.

> His forehead, that I once thought so manly, and that I now
> think so diabolical, was shaded with a heavy cloud; his basilisk
> eyes were nearly quenched with sleeplessness – and weeping,
> perhaps, for the lashes were wet then; his lips devoid of their
> ferocious sneer, and sealed in an expression of unspeakable
> sadness. (ch. XVII)

Thomas Moser has pointed out how – in his view – the circum-
stances and imagery of the encounters between Heathcliff and
Linton betray an underlying – perhaps unconscious – sexuality.[15]
In the most violent of them, before Catherine's dissociation,
Edgar is physically worsted, and his inadequacy is implied by
Catherine's furious outburst against him. There is a struggle
during which a key is thrown into the hottest part of the fire.
Catherine rings the bell 'until it broke with a twang . . .' 'It was
enough to try the temper of a saint,' relates Mrs Dean, 'such senseless wicked rages. There she lay dashing her head against the arm
of the sofa and grinding her teeth so that you might fancy she
would crash them to splinters!' (ch. XI).

After this Catherine locks her bedroom door, against Mrs Dean
it is stated, but by implication against her husband. The presence
of a sexual element in this and other scenes is natural enough, and
thus no grounds for smirks at the expense of 'Emily Jane'. But
here it may give an awkward impression of involuntary revelation,
and direct the attention from the truth of the work to the individual stresses of the author.

(The last encounter with Heathcliff, however, is deeply impressive as an imaginative realisation of an extraordinary situation;
it certainly has tragic force. After this, their haunting of each
other seems almost inevitable.

'Let me alone. Let me alone,' sobbed Catherine. 'If I've done wrong, I'm dying for it. It is enough! You left me too; but I won't upbraid you! I forgive you. Forgive me!'

'It is hard to forgive, and to look at those eyes, and feel those wasted hands,' he answered. 'Kiss me again; and don't let me see your eyes! I forgive what you have done to me. I love my murderer – but *yours*! How can I?' (ch. xv)

Nevertheless, in their embrace there is a suggestion of de-humanisation: they meet like natural forces, destructively.)

The Freudian interpretation of *Wuthering Heights* now approximates to a received judgement. At its least favourable, it presents Catherine's relationship to Heathcliff as a wish-fulfilment fantasy. So the book is thus limited by and painfully representative of the social conditions of its age: the symptoms apparent in the Brontë male characters are pathological (Ian Watt)[16] and an abandonment of the novelist's proper business. At its most favourable, the situation is seen as an allegory of the individual's relationship with his or her Id: it is ambivalent; Heathcliff is both 'a pitiless, wolfish man' and 'more myself than I am'; he is dreaded as more destructive than beneficial, but he cannot be denied. Seen this way, Catherine and Heathcliff provide no statement about relationships of character, of either a realistic or an ideal kind. Catherine's 'Nelly, I *am* Heathcliff' can be heard as a cry from the prison of the self rather than as an expression of love. (It would, perhaps, be more accurately 'Heathcliff is me'.) 'I am I' is the finding of the classic analysts of love, and relationships must begin there. In this intricately constructed and schematic novel there certainly is some evidence of failure of objectivity and of personal struggle, just as there is in 'The Philosopher'. In the deepest sense, it is autobiographical.

The situation of the heroine here and in *Jane Eyre* has been compared with that of Clarissa, in Richardson's novel. The Clarissa-complex was part of the Victorian feminine outlook; it is apparent even in such a realist work as *Daniel Deronda*, in which the Byronic Grandcourt shows the same effortless power and Satanic inevitability as Heathcliff. Catherine undergoes a sort of violation, followed by a spiritual progress, in which petulant outbursts of jealousy and frustration give way to calm, until she is seen

at the open window, with her hair cut short like that of a
novice.

> but when she was calm, there seemed unearthly beauty in the
> change. The flash of her eyes had been succeeded by a dreamy
> and melancholy softness: they no longer gave the impression of
> looking at the objects round her; they appeared always to gaze
> beyond and far beyond – you would have said out of this
> world. (ch. xv)

Before this transfiguration she is perpetually on one side or the
other of a threshold of sublimation. It is a creative relationship.
'Where Id once was, there shall Ego be.'

To look at another, but related, aspect, the taboo on direct presentation of sexual relationships in Victorian novels often resulted
in incongruity, but in *Wuthering Heights* it produces an element –
detectable if not obvious – of uncertainty in the relationships of
the characters. In this meticulously designed novel, the more
closely one reads the less definite in certain respects is what is hap-
pening. In the final encounter between the lovers Heathcliff
gathers Catherine to him 'with greedy jealousy' when she is preg-
nant. 'For on her existence', we have been told, 'depended that of
another.' After this, the birth of a 'puny, seven months child' is
no surprise. But whose child is it? The doubt arises because of this
reference to its prematurity. Emily Brontë's habit of indicating
the passing of time by hints is familiar from C. P. Sanger's well-
known study, *The Structure of Wuthering Heights*. Heathcliff has had
abundant opportunity to be with Catherine, 'he gradually
established his right to be expected', despite Edgar's dislike of
him, and the child is born about seven months after his return.
(The period is from September of one year to March or there-
abouts of the following.) The child, Cathy, is described as unwanted and friendless at first.

If the child is Heathcliff's, then her later marriage is to her
half-brother, Linton Heathcliff. But she may be the offspring of
a totally incestuous union, if, as has been suggested,[17] Heathcliff
is not a foundling, but an illegitimate son of Mr Earnshaw. One
remembers the latter's excessive protectiveness and his wife's dislike of Heathcliff. The first theory, that the child is Heathcliff's,

can be taken some way, but there are contradictions: Cathy is very much a child of Linton and Catherine, in character and appearance, and in the affectionate relationship with her father that develops. Even a 'notional violation' requires a considerable assault on the narrative. The second, concerning Heathcliff's relationship to Mr Earnshaw, is merely ingenious. Why introduce such a mystery that has no denouement, and merely makes the novel more ambiguous? It has been put forward, however, that there is a suggestion, a metaphoric incest in that Heathcliff and Catherine, if not brother and sister, have been brought up as such. Another incongruity of a kind more conventional in Victorian novels occurs when Heathcliff elopes with Isabella and brings her back to Wuthering Heights. He furiously declares that the key of their room shall not come into her possession: she is to be Edgar's 'proxy in suffering'. If this is a sadistic denial of conjugal rights, well and good, since Heathcliff is dedicated to vengeance – his motive for the marriage – but the plot requires that she have a child by him. It has been pointed out that Heathcliff's presence is enough to provoke a marriage into fertility.[18] The key is only one of many sex symbols; Hindley's pistol-cum-flick-knife is another. Psychological criticism has reanimated the early ghosts of morbidity, if not of perversion, in *Wuthering Heights*.

The known predicament of an author can be transcended in the achieved subject of a work, and their relationship is important when considering the Brontës (Charlotte, perhaps, more than Emily). Undoubtedly there is a deeply personal, unconscious, or daemonic element in *Wuthering Heights*, just as there is in the work of Strindberg, and of Lawrence. But, though the central situation must be seen as autobiographical, this does not exclude its truth in wider terms. The mere treatment of such subject-matter at this period is certainly evidence of great originality. Such psycho-drama has its own truth, and is a valid subject of art. *Wuthering Heights* may have diverged from its author's intentions, but this central allegory is realised with great artistic power. It is echoed or reflected in the whole structure of the book, which manifests not an ethically valid view of life, but an artistically effective one.

As a whole, *Wuthering Heights* reveals not pathological inco-
herence, but abundant evidence of conscious, intellectual control.
It is, perhaps, unique for its time among English novels in that
a strictly rationalist view of human life as part of nature is one of
its organising principles. To consider an aspect already briefly
referred to, and which not only reflects, but also, in a sense, con-
tradicts the central situation: the schematic view of life of this
tempestuous novel is formally symbolic of the theme of self-
fulfilment in its various aspects. The main groups of characters
and their settings exemplify the widely disseminated Spinozism
of the period; they are divided into those who ask of life *laetitia*
(happiness) and those who are content with *titillatio* (pleasure).
Catherine's tragedy is precipitated, as the dialogue with Nelly
Dean shows, by her choice of the second. She is, however, an
exception, partaking of both worlds.

Otherwise the characters are obsessively consistent. Not they to
be found, like Stendhal's Julien Sorel, in situations where all their
ideas change; according to Spinoza's view of the world, they 'per-
sist in their own being'. When Emily Brontë gives them time to
reflect, their enduring traits are revealed. For instance in the
famous contrasting ideas of heaven of the younger Catherine and
Linton (which I need hardly quote). In this instance the schematisation conflicts with the mood: such a sympathetic passage as
Linton's view of a tranquil heaven (his Thrushcross side) is quite
out of place on the lips of this petulant character: 'We've allus
summut uh orther side', says Joseph. This is only one dilemma of
the attempt to reconcile the moods of the human psyche with a
scientific typology. Emily Brontë's naturalism has something in
common with Balzac's view of society and Zola's tainted families.
Romantic Spinozism certainly cleared the ground for truths about
human life, but the further dilemma of reconciling a naturalist
view with certain aspects of human nature, such as the religious
consciousness, is apparent in the philosophy of Spinoza himself
(if his exegetes* are to be relied on) and it is common in romanticism which he so greatly influenced. It is certainly apparent in

---

* For instance J. A. Froude, and D. G. James in *The Romantic Comedy*.

Wuthering Heights. Catherine and Heathcliff are, through the structure of the book, identified with nature, and their love is expressed in a way which suggests the inevitability of a natural force, so it is difficult – on this view – to see what specifically human or ideal significance can be attached to it. But Catherine does not conform, she is a pathetically divided being. The same dilemma is discernible in Blake, whose cult of energy and moral outlook have something in common with Emily Brontë's. However, one effect of the organisation of *Wuthering Heights* is a strong emphasis on psychological necessity and – in a paradoxical way – human individuality, the predestination of character. The view seems to anticipate much in modern psychology and anthropology.

In the dance or allegory of energy of *Wuthering Heights*, there is one nonconformist element, Catherine, and she is crushed by it. Her consciousness is not restricted to nature. (Even in her less worldly moments, her emotion is strongly egotistical, however.)

> Nelly, you think you are better and more fortunate than I; in full health and strength – you are sorry for me – very soon that will be altered. I shall be sorry for *you*. I shall be incomparably beyond and above you all. (ch. xv)

The surface piety or religiosity of the Lintons is constantly challenged. Catherine's dilemma is at the centre of *Wuthering Heights*, and it is that of humanity. Total fulfilment is impossible, not because of social convention, but by the terms of life. The romanticism of the novel tends to a powerful death-wish, with the fact of death seen both as leading to possible fulfilment and simply as release, oblivion. It is a predominantly pessimistic view.

It is in accord with the high romantic aspect that Heathcliff should die of love for Catherine, but he proceeds to a final (suggested) union with her in more than one sense; he takes over her role. The embodiment of vengeance loses interest in his worldly designs and his feeling for Catherine becomes mystical, and an annihilation of the body. Meanwhile the more conventional romance between Hareton and Cathy develops. Is *Wuthering Heights* to be considered as a tragedy that unsatisfactorily dwindles into a story of regeneration? The ending, it has been suggested, denotes not a resolution of the theme, but an abandonment of it.[19] There is a suggestion, perhaps, of the Brontë retreat from dangerous romanticism into domesticity. Emily Brontë had to end her novel acceptably, but this would not excuse a failure of art.

The presence of Cathy and Hareton perhaps implies

> we that are young
> Shall never see so much . . .

Such attempts to bisect the work must also take account of the enduring consciousness of Heathcliff and Catherine, through Emily Brontë's use of the supernatural, not for specious mystification or atmosphere, but to suggest the possibility of personal immortality. The younger pair may be unaware of them, but they haunt the work to the end, to the final sentence: 'and wondered how any one could ever imagine unquiet slumbers, for the sleepers in that quiet earth'. 'In view of what we know of Heathcliff, perpetually vibrant with passion, and of Cathy, ceaselessly haunting him, we must find this passage profoundly ironic', writes Thomas Moser. 'There is, however, no evidence that Emily Brontë perceived that irony.'[20]

The passage is spoken by Lockwood, who is unable to imagine anything much, so it is ambiguous. But again one suspects that the author is not committing herself, and how, in this connection, should she? The end of *Wuthering Heights* is beautiful and appropriate. At the very least, in meeting the conflicting requirements of a conventional ending and her artistic conscience, Emily Brontë's touch was never surer. The redemption theme is anticipated in the poems.

Much more could be said – though a great deal already has been – about Emily Brontë's *écriture*, as also about the admirable poetic unity of *Wuthering Heights*. Maugham wrote that 'the whole book is very badly written in the pseudo-literary manner that the amateur is apt to affect'. Leaving aside the question of his authority in this connection, one feels that he was mistaking Lockwood's style for his creator's. Emily Brontë's plain style is admirable and dateless – unlike that of most Victorian novels – while her great manner has a Dantean splendour to which few, if any, parallels are available in the prose literature of the period. 'I dreamt I was sleeping the last sleep, by that sleeper, with my heart stopped, and my cheek frozen against hers.'

A first reading of *Wuthering Heights* is a unique experience in more than mere logic, but on subsequent readings it will be more apparent that the tempest of the opening, and that which accompanies the separation of the lovers, becomes the 'soft wind' of the close, and that the sun and moon, the fierce and the passive, are momentarily present together in the 'beamless amber light along the west' of Lockwood's last visit.

Wuthering Heights is not among the masterpieces in which a rigid moral code operates and the statement is weighed and final; for all its artistic autonomy it is personal and about conflict, protest and growth; it answers few questions and asks many. The exploration it represents was the work of a great executive of the novel, a system-builder. In the enclosed space of *Wuthering Heights* all life (round the centre of disturbance) conforms to dominant principles of contrast.

BOOK THREE

Public and Critics: 1846-1968

AT FIRST Emily Brontë was known to the public only as the pseudonymous poet Ellis Bell, contributor to a joint volume, then as pseudonymous novelist, considered by some reviewers not to exist in her own right, but to be a younger Currer Bell, by others to be indistinguishable from Currer Bell. She then emerged, though still partly in the shadows, as the Emily Brontë, the 'unobtrusive woman' of her sister's 1850 prefaces, later the difficult but powerful character of Mrs Gaskell's *Life of Charlotte Brontë*. The heroine half of the image, early established, has proved permanent, but assessment of the writer based on any sort of real understanding of her work has had to wait until the present century.

Had the Brontës been more professional, in the pejorative sense, their first offering would probably have been fiction, rather than a small volume of poetry. The 1840s did not provide a general seller's market for poetry, despite its greater prestige than fiction in certain quarters. A growing social conscience put a premium on the literary form that best embodied the working of society. There was a glut of poetry, particularly by women. Their choice of neutral pen-names does, however, look professional or extremely prudent in the light of such evidence as a piece of female doggerel published in the *World of Fashion* in 1840.

> Oh Colburn, Murray, Longman, in pity come and buy
> And transmit our unrivalled lays unto posterity.
> We cannot pay a publisher, we sit us down and weep.

The Brontës were published, initially, only because they could pay. When *Tait's Edinburgh Magazine* (July 1846) noted *Poems by Currer, Ellis and Acton Bell* in its 'Literary Register' it was with the comment that 'new poems multiply so rapidly we are hardly able to catalogue their names'. A lively London weekly, the *Critic*, in one of the very few reviews of the first (Aylott and Jones) edition of the *Poems*, found the volume refreshing after the 'heaps of trash and trumpery that lumber the table of the literary journalist.'[1]

A few favourable – in Emily Brontë's case highly favourable – reviews gave encouragement, as Charlotte's letters reveal, though they did not result in sales. The most successful poetry of the decade, the long narrative poems such as Arthur Hugh Clough's *Bothie* and Tennyson's *The Princess*, tended to resemble novels. Lyric poetry, however 'simple', 'native' and 'fresh' (these were the reviewers' favourite labels for the Brontës' poems), after that of Mrs Hemans, and by unknown writers, was unlikely to achieve wide recognition. (Later, interest in the Brontës became a cumulative thing, to which their works *in toto* and the story of their lives contributed.) The 1850 *Wuthering Heights* was published with eighteen previously unpublished poems by Emily, including 'No coward soul is mine'; their poetical value was 'next to naught' according to G. H. Lewes, though not all the reviewers agreed with him; but by 1857, after publication of *The Life of Charlotte Brontë*, reviewers were again quoting her poems. Some journalists, such as W. C. Roscoe, took the opportunity of reminding readers that she was underrated as a poet;[2] others began to detect the affinities with her novel.

Wuthering Heights has become something of a standard by which the taste – the aesthetic and critical climate of its period – has been judged. There is a widespread belief that it was either ignored, condemned or 'carried' by *Jane Eyre*. Such views were first fostered by the tragic note of Charlotte Brontë's prefaces, her very qualified praise and overshadowing fame, and they need some modification in the light of the contemporary press. *Wuthering Heights* led an independent, if stormy, existence: it was neither understood nor ignored.

Our own preoccupation with media and communication and our understanding of the striking influence of convention on the functioning of an art form in a given period make the baffled awe that was the average Victorian reaction to *Wuthering Heights* easier to understand. It was not only a question of morality, but of a new relationship – in which, of course, morality was involved – between novelist and reader. Seen through spectacles that polarise light, the world appears inverted, but after a time the wearer's vision returns to normal. It took an unusually long time – more than half a century – for *Wuthering Heights* to look even approximately the right way up. The book offended accepted standards of tone, technique and subject-matter, but its power was undeniable. Whereas *Jane Eyre*, the nearest comparison to hand, was widely praised for its truth and its 'realism' – a judgement time has confirmed, with qualifications – *Wuthering Heights* was considered an altogether stranger, more provocative, work. The formal aspects that now seem most interesting were, as might be expected, the least understood. (Closely related subjects in poetry caused no such difficulties.) There is something very characteristic of the period in this determination to eat *Wuthering Heights* and have it too. But the more perceptive critics, Dobell, Lewes, Roscoe and Masson, can be seen moving towards a view of fiction that could accommodate such works (as their reviews of *Wuthering Heights* show). Dramatisation – in the Jamesian sense – and artistic autonomy were increasingly, if still insufficiently, appreciated. Charlotte Brontë was urged to admire Jane Austen by G. H. Lewes in early 1848.[3] On the other hand, the author–reader relationship, strengthened by the interactions of serialisation, was generally closer than when Jane Austen wrote and there was a new and larger readership for fiction. Like *Madame Bovary*, *Wuthering Heights* notably deprived the reader of this comfort, usually that of being preached to. To read Lewes on *Wilhelm Meister* is to wonder that the *kunstlerischer Atheismus* of *Wuthering Heights* was not better appreciated, but is also to see why.

Robert Hall [a well-known preacher] confessed that reading Miss Edgeworth hindered him for a week in his clerical functions; he was completely disturbed by her pictures of a world of happy, active people *without* any visible interference of religion.[4]

The best standards demanded a faithful rendering of experience, but only of certain sectors of it. What R. Stang, in *The Theory of*

162

Emily Brontë

the Novel in England, has called the Procrustes' bed of realism into which most reviewers tried to fit *Wuthering Heights* led to many inconsistencies.[5] 'Plot of the story there is none', V. H. Hobart wrote, surprisingly.[6] Many critics considered that the book portrayed 'real' people, but that such characters should not be introduced into fiction. Standards had certainly grown out of the 'make 'em laugh, make 'em cry, make 'em wait' stage, but even Lewes was prepared to attack the recondite, the search for hidden meanings, as an unhealthy preoccupation of German philosophic criticism[7] (though fortunately, unlike many contemporaries, he did not adhere to his own principle). So it is not surprising that *Wuthering Heights* did not get the close reading that alone could lead to juster appreciation.

A factor in the acceptance of *Wuthering Heights* for publication was probably Emily Brontë's successful use of her romantic models. Charlotte's *The Professor* was refused the same year, for 'want of thrilling incident'. *Wuthering Heights* appeared (accidentally perhaps, since Newby probably delayed publication until *Jane Eyre* was a success) as a Christmas book. It was listed under 'Books Received' in the *Critic*, 4 December 1847. The first edition sold out, according to Charlotte's correspondence with Smith, Elder, when they were producing a second edition, regardless of Newby's claims.[8]

Wuthering Heights evidently enjoyed a certain notoriety from the first. Its impact was considerable, particularly, it seems, in certain circles in America where it appeared within a few months.

our object [commented the *American Review*] has been simply to warn the young, whom these ideal personages of *Wuthering Heights* are so strongly impressing, against the infection of unconsciously imitating them. Let no hopeless young gentleman persevere in a constancy like Heathcliff's![9]

Here was a Boston *Werther*!

Many reviewers raised (inadequately) critical issues still very alive. Emily Brontë's narrative was admired in pictorial terms, such as 'keeping' and 'chiaroscuro'. Nor was the quality of her writing in detail entirely neglected.

* * *

Emily Brontë died just a year after publication of *Wuthering Heights*. Her sister, and – by undeniable right – literary executor, survived her by six and a half years. Neither these circumstances, nor the general temper of the period were to prove entirely favourable to her as a writer. It is intriguing but indeterminate to consider how her reputation might have fared on its own. The status and influence of Currer Bell helped to make Ellis/Emily known, but the Emily she promoted was seen through the eyes of a remarkable writer of penetrating but narrow critical outlook. As A. R. Brick has pointed out, 'the author of *Jane Eyre*, effectual leader of Emily and Anne while they lived, was now proprietress of their reputations, which she would have neither under- nor over-valued'.[10] By the end of 1850 Charlotte had met Harriet Martineau, Lewes, Mrs Gaskell and Matthew Arnold. Public interest in the works of all the Bells grew with the celebrity of Currer, with her further works and pronouncements, and with her presence on the literary scene.

In a sense Emily Brontë's public existence had commenced, her personality had made itself felt in its own distinctive way, when she did not accompany her sisters on their visit to Charlotte's publisher, George Smith, much earlier, in 1848. (The cause of this well-known epiphany was Newby's offer of Anne Brontë's second work to an American publisher under the false colours of a new work by Currer Bell.) Charlotte's subsequent appeals to her publishers to conceal Ellis Bell's identity, soon followed by her account of her death, must have aroused curiosity. But her identity was not known to the general public until Charlotte's prefaces appeared in the memorial edition of *Wuthering Heights* in late 1850.

Sydney Dobell's well-known notice was published in the *Palladium* (September 1850) three months before this edition. It was nominally a review of *Shirley*, but much of it was devoted to *Wuthering Heights*, which – despite Charlotte Brontë's disclaimer in the third edition of *Jane Eyre* – he believed to be an early work of hers. *Shirley*, he considered, showed a falling-off from the imaginative power of *Wuthering Heights*, which threw him, like other writers, into contradictory attitudes: his enthusiastic praise still denied it the title of work of art, while he acknowledged effects that could only have resulted from considerable art. (Dobell's recognition that *Jane Eyre's* high place was already assured is worth noting. It had been reviewed much more widely than *Wuthering Heights*. A factor here was perhaps the Smith, Elder organisation behind *Jane Eyre*, the publicity pull that Sadleir has suggested Emily's publisher, Newby, lacked. Many notices of *Jane Eyre* were in provincial papers that *Wuthering Heights* never reached.)

The memorial edition of the latter appeared in December 1850, published by Smith, Elder, who took it over willy-nilly from the defaulting Newby. It included Charlotte's Biographical Notice of her sisters and her critical Preface. In this prefatory matter she used, for the first time in print, her sisters' first names, as well as the curious asexual pen-names. She might, one feels, have accompanied her qualified praise of their works with a selection of favourable reviews – cuttings of which were available at the parsonage – a service performed for the reprints of *Jane Eyre* by the same publisher. But she did not arrange this.

The resulting reviews of this popular, one-volume edition reveal the growing interest in the lives of the authors. A three-and-a-quarter-column article in the *Athenaeum*[11] maintained earlier hostility to *Wuthering Heights*, referring to 'isolated women' and not going even as far as Charlotte in qualified praise. Her Preface was 'an argument, if not a defence, the urgency of which is not sufficiently admitted by the bulk of readers'. Since Ellis Bell did not understand real people, she had to delineate a 'self-consistent monster'. The *Economist* had already given *Wuthering Heights* a paragraph or two, and now it accepted Charlotte's moderate valuation of the two reprinted works and suggested that the pathetic story of the authors, as told by their sister, would lead to a new interest in them.[12] Writing in the *Leader*,[13] Lewes considered *Wuthering Heights* a work of genius, but immature and crude. (Writing to James Taylor of Smith, Elder a few days later, Charlotte preferred the *Athenaeum* notice; perhaps she could not accept Lewes's admiration for such a creation as Heathcliff.[14]) Lewes's failure to appreciate the form of the book is a measure of how far it was misunderstood, even by the most intelligent of contemporary readers. He suggested that earlier praise (in journals such as the *Britannia* and *Atlas*) was too generous, but his own shows the then common dilemma of sensibility in conflict with preconceptions as to the realist and didactic function of the novel. In this, among the most penetrating of the early notices, Lewes shrewdly related the Brontës' subject-matter to their situation (of which a little was now revealed), and sensed the urgent personal experience behind their works. He was among the earliest critics to see the importance of the divided character of Catherine.

The identity of 'W.P.P.', author of the monograph *Jottings on Currer, Ellis and Acton Bell* (1856) is still unknown, but he was aware that Mrs Gaskell was working on a commissioned biography. He (less likely, she) endorsed the accepted order of preference for the Brontës, considering that Charlotte had brought about a revolution in literature, but also that the creator of Heathcliff must be 'a god among writers'. This enthusiasm was shared in the early 1850s by Dante Gabriel Rossetti and the religious writer, Dr J. Brown, who placed *Wuthering Heights* above *Jane Eyre*.[15]

In being more than a pious memoirist or editor, Mrs Gaskell broke new ground in contemporary biography, indeed *The Life of Charlotte Brontë* shows an appealing naïvety in dealing frankly with recent sources and living persons. So the interest it aroused was more than literary. In satisfying the curiosity aroused by Charlotte's prefaces as to the background and characters of the Brontës, the *Life* added little to critical understanding of the works themselves. Its reviewers, however, seemed irresistibly drawn to the subject of *Wuthering Heights* and to its author's poetry. Unable to analyse *Wuthering Heights*, they were nevertheless able to appreciate in some measure its disturbing intensity. In some instances, aware of the dominance of personality compared with characterisation in *Wuthering Heights*, they drew conclusions about its author missed by Mrs Gaskell. They anticipated most interestingly some recent critical issues. The *Blackwood's* critic (it was Eneas Sweetland Dallas) noticed that 'good Mrs Gaskell, who has a basis of firm self-esteem to go upon', failed to bring out the sensitivity and pessimism behind Emily Brontë's social personality.[16] He recognised that Heathcliff is an allegorical figure as much as a character from life. In a long essay in the *National Review* W. C. Roscoe combined horrified strictures on the brutality of the book ('We cannot help shrinking, from a mind which could conceive and describe, even in a dream, the rubbing backwards and forwards of a child's hand along the jagged glass . . .') with awed admiration of its power.[17] Like Lewes, he was troubled with realist preconceptions. The subjectivity of *Wuthering Heights* threatened characterisation and probability. For V. H. Hobart it was a primitive, drawn from life, and with profound psychological truth.[18] Peter Bayne was also contradictory and uncertain of the final place of *Wuthering Heights*, but, virtually alone among mid-century critics, he sensed that there was more to it than imaginative power, glimpsing the essential function of control and viewpoint.[19]

The *Life of Charlotte Brontë* also attracted some attention on the Continent. In *La Revue des Deux Mondes* Emile Montégut suggested a similarity between *Wuthering Heights* and the work of Hoffmann. The plot was strange, he wrote, but it was treated without hypocrisy or false reticence. Emily Brontë's characters were criminal, but she defied the reader not to admire them.[20] In 1860 *Le Moniteur universel* described it (with echoes of Baudelaire, published in 1857?) as 'une fleur malade'. But such comments were incidental to a principal interest in Charlotte Brontë, as *Jane Eyre* very quickly had a European reputation.

If *Wuthering Heights* was still a curiosity, the will, stoicism and independence manifest in Emily Brontë's life and in her poems had a less equivocal appeal for the mid-Victorians. She began to be recognised as the least sociable but most Promethean of the family. Mrs Gaskell's letters reveal that, privately, she was more impressed than she allowed in the *Life*.[21] The Brontës and, one imagines, Emily in particular, were an inspiration to Emily Dickinson in America. Matthew Arnold's fine 'Haworth Churchyard' was written before Mrs Gaskell's work appeared. One suspects a real influence on Arnold; there is certainly a shared romantic pantheism apparent in his early poem 'A Wish' and originating in a common feeling for nature. Emily Brontë, in her portrayal of the most 'savage race' in Victorian literature ('I wish

I were a child again, half savage . . .'), felt, and perhaps in turn influenced, the undercurrent of nostalgia for the primitive under the first threats of affluence. There is little, if any, direct evidence of her influence on Victorian novels (except perhaps on her sisters'), but such a character as Bradley Headstone – the name is suggestive – in *Our Mutual Friend* is related to Heathcliff. Influence n Swinburne (an admitted admirer of *Wuthering Heights*), in *The Cross Currents of Love*, has been suggested. *Wuthering Heights* was seldom reprinted until released from copyright, since when there has been an average of one edition every two years, if one includes translations. There seems to be no critic of the first rank to be turned to for more than an aside on *Wuthering Heights* during the nineteenth century. For most readers it remained a curiosity. Ford Madox Ford, remembering in the thirties his mother's admiration of it, explained that her taste was advanced.[22] In 1897 the critic of the *Daily Mail* referred to *Wuthering Heights* in a review of *Dracula*.[23] For the minor literary historians of the latter half of the nineteenth century and after – Robertson, Walker, Miles and Chesterton – Emily Brontë was still primarily the poet and heroine. The esoteric character of *Wuthering Heights* is indicated by Henry James's neglect of it when he suggested that the real artistic coming-of-age of the English novel was not until the eighties.[24] His well-founded distaste for the taint of immoderate biography that clung to the Brontës may have been the cause of his unfair neglect of this – on recent showing – most *discutable* of novels. Leslie Stephen, on the lines of his predecessors of the 1850s, took the definition of the essential difference between the two Brontës a little further. ('The sisters indeed differed widely, though with a strong resemblance. The iron had not entered so deeply into Charlotte's nature. . . . She [Emily] feels rather than observes, while Charlotte feels in observing.'[25]) But his rationalist position precluded any enlightenment concerning *Wuthering Heights*, and led to a repetition of the charge of defective art. Nevertheless – it is a matter of tone – one prefers Stephen on the Brontës to almost anyone else in the century. Emily Brontë's fastidious isolation and detachment make any suggested resemblance to the *fin de siècle* type of womanhood rather far-fetched, but intellectually, perhaps, the parallel is possible. Swinburne appreciatively reviewed Mary Robinson's *Emily Brontë* (1883), one of a series on 'Eminent Women'; for him the at that time accepted confusion of *Wuthering Heights* was 'external or accidental' not 'inward and spiritual'.[26] Arthur Symons[27] often admired Emily Brontë and wrote a preface to the first separate edition of her poems (1906). George Saintsbury's assessment, like many others, is patronising ('it would be unreasonable to expect perfection of method') and does not really advance understanding of *Wuthering Heights*, but his critical prose has sensitive antennae and provides a curious anticipation of Professor Leavis on the Brontës.

> If *Wuthering Heights* had stood alone [surely it did] it would have continued to be more or less alone – a kind of 'sport' as botanists say, in the nineteenth century as Beckford's *Vathek* is in the late eighteenth, a wonderful and isolated *tour de force* very unlikely to be in any way germinal, to found a school, and still more unlikely to revolutionise.[28]

Wuthering Heights began to be seen in the context of romanticism as much as of the mainstream of the novel; the idea was hardly developed, but is certainly present, in the preface by Mrs Humphry Ward, on whom Emily Brontë was a strong personal influence and inspiration. The dual process of rediscovery, and redispersal of Brontëana, commencing with Shorter's purchases from Arthur Nicholls, resulted, on balance, in a wider basis for modern studies.

The stage of defence of Emily Brontë as an artist (the essays by David Cecil, C. P. Sanger, etc.) in the modern period has given way to one of interpretation. The rediscovery of *Wuthering Heights* has a rough analogy in the rediscovery of Elizabethan drama by romantic critics or in the increased understanding of the problems presented by such a work as *Hamlet*. It has been partly a matter of warier reading, of alertness to the hidden nature of works produced under cultural restraint or influenced by personal conflict ('The teacher's first job', writes Professor Trilling, 'is to lead his students to accept what is odd'), and, above all, of better understanding of the subtleties of fiction as an art that can present experience in many ways, of which direct imitation is only one. In this process the special contribution of American critics should not be underestimated (though one often wishes they would present their findings in simpler language). Emily Brontë's reputation has grown relatively more than that of Dickens or George Eliot during the twentieth century; she has been very much an interest of the modern sensibility. I do not think that this is so much a matter of her social consciousness as has been suggested, for such consciousness was general among her contemporaries, but more of artistic rigour, extremism, and of the kinds of experience that interested her most – the instincts and the Promethean consciousness of man. But the esoteric character of *Wuthering Heights*, its violence, suggestions of perversity, subjectivity and the personal alienation of its author have a modish appeal that has led . to some misplacement of emphasis and to neglect of her more positive and life-enhancing qualities, such as an essential respect for nature (how relevant now!) and for life. The continuing supply of papers on various aspects of *Wuthering Heights* is a tribute to its richness, but the conflicting opinions as to its central meaning and intention are signs of an unusually controversial work.

'Out of her a minor tradition comes,' Professor Leavis has written,[29] citing George Douglas's small masterpiece, *The House with the Green Shutters*. Though this shares the romantic concern for fineness of feeling and perception in conflict with unpropitious circumstances, the *scale* of concern in *The House with the Green Shutters*, as a regional domestic tragedy, is much less, as is its technical interest. This minor tradition appears in rather unimportant works, modern romantic novels which show structural parallels. (Aspects of the book – or of imitations of it – were successfully satirised in *Cold Comfort Farm*.)

Emily Brontë would, I think, be as interesting a writer – if a less well understood one – on the strength of *Wuthering Heights* alone. She is not a very strong candidate for the still-vacant position of major English poet who is also female, but on the other hand one cannot exactly call those lines from 'The Prisoner' and such a poem as 'No coward soul is mine' minor poetry.

Mrs Browning's sophistication and facility are preferable to much of the clouded landscape of the Gondal poems, but she wrote nothing with such attack as these. The problem is apparent in the last edition of *The Cambridge Bibliography of English Literature*, which refused Emily Brontë a place among nineteenth-century poets, but – reluctant to classify her as minor – evaded the issue with a cross-reference to novelists. The general level of her work comes off badly in comparison with that of Emily Dickinson. W. H. Auden has however included her in an anthology of nineteenth-century minor poets.[30] She satisfies only one of his five conditions for the major poet, in showing an 'unmistakeable originality of vision and style' (in a few poems only), and two of the five (scope of output and organic development of an *œuvre*) she hardly had time to fulfil.

'It is tempting to retort there is only one Brontë.'[31] Yielding (some way) to this temptation and thus setting the two most important Brontës at odds is an invidious but perhaps necessary process. As writers they come first to mind as manifesting some of the main tendencies of romanticism in English fiction. (Indeed, Emily Brontë tends to blur the distinction between prose fiction and poetry.) But the conflict in their works between romanticism and other values more stable, domestic and conventional is also important. Emily, in her novel and to some extent in her poems, shows this conflict at its most bitter; she was the most 'Brontë' of the Brontës. As novelist she reveals her greatness, compared with Charlotte, in among other things her complete freedom from autobiography, from the raw use of personal experience, and in her intellectual power. Charlotte Brontë's qualities are closely related to those of her letters, and Emily wrote almost none. It is, perhaps, more difficult to answer the questions raised by this social harshness than in the parallel case of Emily Dickinson, of whom a recent critic has written:

Yet how far this paradox of gain-through-loss represented an actual triumph of life for Emily Dickinson is another matter. Richard Wilbur in a brilliant paper calls it 'emotional strategy'. It belonged with the love story to the realm of her imaginative explorations. While agreeing that in her philosophy of abstention she arrived at a profound truth about the human soul, one may doubt, from the biographical point of view, whether she derived much joy or satisfaction from it.[32]

The conflict between the claims of passion and the social order is only one element in Emily Brontë's work, and not the most important. She raises the conflict to another plane, the last redoubt of the romantic attitude, where the individual confronts the human situation at its most tragic. Revealed religion was still a sufficient force in the nineteenth century to give the Victorian questioning of it a special intensity. The search for the supernatural sometimes took bizarre forms, but Emily Brontë – if one cares to look at her in this way – provides a striking example of it, and one which puts her intellectually with the male writers of her generation. She could inhabit, artistically, the obscure area where passion and the religious consciousness are almost indistinguishable. She also alternates a strong feeling for 'nature and the language of the sense' with *Weltschmerz* and denial of life. The romantic's paradise lost is a terrestrial one, and if Emily Brontë's mystical tendency made life seem transitory and illusory, her romanticism made it all too real. She was able to express these themes, in one work at least, with a power and originality that give it a place in world literature. This was hardly a career cut short: Emily Brontë's qualities, rather like those of Keats, seem inseparable from her situation; she had just time to make her point.

List of Abbreviations

AB	Anne Brontë
BPM	Brontë Parsonage Museum.
BST	*Brontë Society Transactions*
CB	Charlotte Brontë
DA	*Dissertation Abstracts*
EB	Emily Brontë
EC	*Essays in Criticism*
EN	Ellen Nussey
ES	*Essays and Studies by Members of the English Association*
KR	*Kenyon Review*
Life	*The Life of Charlotte Brontë*, by Mrs Gaskell, 3rd ed. (1919)
MLR	*Modern Language Review*
NCF	*Nineteenth Century Fiction*
NQ	*Notes and Queries*
PB	Patrick Brontë
PBB	Patrick Branwell Brontë
PMLA	*Proceedings of the Modern Language Association of America*
SHB	Shakespeare Head Brontë (*The Brontës, their Lives, Friendships and Correspondence.* 4 vols)
SHBMU	Shakespeare Head Brontë (*The Miscellaneous and Unpublished Writing of Charlotte and Patrick Branwell Brontë*)
TLS	*Times Literary Supplement*
WSW	W. S. Williams

A Location List of Manuscripts

THE POEMS

No additional poems by EB have been found since Hatfield's edition, published in 1941. His Introduction includes a detailed account of how the authentic text and corpus of the poems were established.

All but sixteen of the poems in this edition are printed from the original manuscripts. Fourteen out of this sixteen, the Hatfield 'J' poems, were printed from Shorter's transcripts, and Hatfield was unable to find the originals. None of them as printed has heading initials or signature or positive Gondal indication to support the ascription, and one – H128 – is now known to be by CB (M. G. Christian's Census). So in the light of Shorter's record as editor they cannot be considered as reliable as the rest. Though Hatfield's Introduction is an implicit condemnation of him, they were co-editors of the SHB, and his inclusion of these poems goes a long way in their favour.

The other poem for which no manuscript has yet been found, 'Often rebuked, but always back returning', was first printed in the 1850 selection prepared by CB. Hatfield suggested that it is by her, but the question remains open.

Miss Christian's Census and W. D. Paden's *An Investigation of Gondal*, both show that Hatfield's edition needs minor revisions. His amendments seem to me occasionally injudicious. For instance, in 'A.G.A. to A.S.' (H61), EB's exclamation 'Can Death – yes, Death, he is thine own!' has been made nonsense by amending 'Can' to 'Call'.

1. The 'Gondal Poems', BritishMuseum, Smith Bequest, Add.MS 43483 (Hatfield 'B' poems), 68 pp., 45 poems. Headed: 'Emily Jane Brontë, Transcribed Feb 1844. Gondal Poems.' The manuscript published, ed. J. Mott and H. Brown (Shakespeare Head Press, 1938).
2. The 'Honresfeld' manuscript, a transcript notebook commenced at the same period as the 'Gondal Poems' manuscript, 29 pp., 31 poems (Hatfield 'A' poems). Sold by T. J. Wise to Sir Alfred Law, and now believed to be in the possession of a descendant. Transcribed in 1926 by Davidson Cook; his account with details of CB's alterations published in *The Nineteenth Century and After* (Aug 1926). No. 1 of three copies of his transcript at BPM. Facsimiles of all the poems in SHB *Poems of EB and AB* (1934).

3. Part of longhand notebook, bound for T. J. Wise, passed to British Museum in Ashley Collection. Ashley MS 175, 24 pp., 16 poems or fragments (Hatfield 'C' poems). Contains alterations by EB, probably made when she prepared the Gondal Poems manuscript.
4. 63 poems and fragments on 12 sheets. Bonnell Collection at BPM. No. 12 in Hatfield catalogue of the Bonnell Collection. Hatfield 'D' poems, 3–16.
5. 4 poems on 2 sheets, originally in Bonnell Collection. Believed presented to Pierpont Morgan Library, 1964, by Mrs Bonnell. Hatfield 'D' poems, 1 and 2.
6. The Howe manuscript, Berg Collection, New York Public Library. 33 poems on 20 sheets. Hatfield 'E' poems, 1–20.
7. 2 poems on 2 sheets. The Texas manuscript, Library of the University of Texas, Austin. Hatfield 'F' poems, 1 and 2.

DIARY PAPERS

1. 24 November 1834, also signed by AB, commencing 'I fed Rainbow, Diamond, Snowflake, Jasper . . .' Bonnell Collection, no. 131, at BPM. Transcript: Ratchford, *Gondal's Queen*, appendixes.
2. Commencing 'Monday evening, June 26, 1837 – A bit past 4-o-clock . . .' Brontë Society Collection at BPM. Christian catalogue of the General Collection, section 3, no. 105. Transcript, Ratchford, op. cit.
3. Birthday note, 30 July 1841, commencing, 'It is Friday evening, near 9 o'clock . . .' Originally in Law Collection, following purchase by C. K. Shorter for T. J. Wise. Probably sold and in private hands in America. Facsimile published in Shorter's *Charlotte Brontë and her Circle* (1896), in SHB, and in *The Complete Works of Emily Jane Brontë*, ed. Shorter (1911). Transcript based on facsimiles, etc., Ratchford, op. cit.
4. Birthday note, 'Haworth, Thursday, July 30, 1845', commencing 'my birthday, showery, breezy, cool . . .' Passed, like 3, into Law Collection. W. Gérin writes: 'Once in Law Collection, dispersed' (*Anne Brontë*). Facsimile of portion in SHB and full text. Text also published in *The Brontës and their Circle*, by Shorter. Facsimile in *The Complete Works of Emily Jane Brontë*, by Shorter. Transcript, Ratchford, op. cit.

ESSAYS AND EXERCISES IN FRENCH

1. 'Le Chat', 15 May 1842. Berg Collection, New York Public Library. English translation by L. Nagel in *Five Essays in French*, ed. F. E. Ratchford (University of Texas Press, 1948).

2. 'Portrait: Le Roi Harold avant la bataille de Hastings', June 1842. Bonnell Collection, BP M. English translation by Nagel, in *Five Essays in French*.
3. 'Lettre. Ma chère Madam . . .', 26 July 1842. Mme Beckers-Heger, 57 Rue Alphonse XIII, Brussels. Facsimile of typed transcript and translation published in *BST* XII, pt 65 (1955).
4. 'Lettre d'un frère à un frère', 5 August 1842. Stark Collection, University of Texas. English translation by Nagel, in *Five Essays in French*.
5. 'L'Amour filial', August 1842. Bonnell Collection, BPM. English translation by D. Cornish, in *BST* XI, pt 57 (1947).
6. 'Le Papillon', 11 August 1842. Berg Collection, New York Public Library. English translation by Nagel, in *Five Essays in French*.
7. 'Palais de la mort', 18 October 1842. Bonnell Collection, BPM. English translation by Nagel, in *Five Essays in French*. Another translation by M. Lane, in *BST* XII, pt 64 (1954).

LETTERS

1. To Ellen Nussey, beginning 'Dear Miss Ellen, I should be wanting in common civility'. Undated, endorsed May 1843. British Museum, Ashley MS 177.
2. To Ellen Nussey, beginning 'Dear Miss Nussey, If you have set your heart on Charlotte staying'. 18 (or 15) July 1845 (or 1843). Signature cut off. BPM, Haworth.
3. To Ellen Nussey, beginning 'Dear Miss Nussey – I fancy this note will be too late'. 25 February 1846 (as printed in SHB). Present location unknown.

A section of the catalogue of the general collection at the BPM prepared by M. G. Christian is devoted to non-literary material relating to EB: some pencil sketches and colour drawings, geometrical diagrams and the remains of an account-book.

An Emily Brontë Reading List

From the bibliographical aspect, the Brontës are almost indivisible, and the literature is, of course, extensive, commencing even before Mrs Gaskell's work in 1857. It is more difficult than is the case with many writers to distinguish between biography and criticism. If one attempts to be comprehensive, a great deal of more or less dead wood (but part of the Brontë phenomenon) must be included.

There is now considerably more criticism of Emily than of Charlotte, but the critical 'best buys' could be narrowed down to a score or so of articles and fewer books. It is sometimes difficult to distinguish between studies of the poems and of the novel. (A work called *The Genesis of Wuthering Heights*, for instance, is mainly concerned with the poems.)

I have tried, nevertheless, to be comprehensive, except for a lunatic fringe, and to group the material according to its kind, textual, biographical and critical. Many studies of 'the Brontës' have, of course, been included, as have outstanding studies of individual Brontës other than Emily.

This bibliography is divided into the following sections:
A. General Works Consulted
B. Editions of Emily Brontë's Works
C. Textual and Bibliographical Studies
D. Biographical Sources and Studies
E. Criticism
F. Studies of the Poems
G. Nineteenth-century Reviews

A. GENERAL WORKS CONSULTED

Aiken, H. D., *The Age of Ideology* (Mentor Philosophers: New York, 1956).
Allen, W., *The English Novel* (Penguin Books: 1958).
Auerbach, E., *Mimesis* (1957).
Baker, E. A., *The History of the English Novel* (1924–39).
Brown, F. K., *Fathers of the Victorians*, reprinted from *Virginia Quarterly Review* (1936).

Chadwick, O., *The Victorian Church*, pt I (1966).

Hayter, A., *Mrs Browning* (1962).

Houghton, W. E., *The Victorian Frame of Mind, 1830–1870* (New Haven, 1957).

James, D. G., *The Romantic Comedy* (1948).

James, L., *Fiction for the Working Man* (1963).

Marcus, S., *Dickens: From Pickwick to Dombey* (1965).

Masson, D., *De Quincey* ('English Men of Letters' series: 1914).

Railo, E., *The Haunted Castle* (1927).

—— *The Reinterpretation of Victorian Literature*, ed. J. E. Baker (1950).

Robson, W. W., 'Byron as Poet', in *Proc. Brit. Acad., 1957* (1958).

Schenk, H. G., *The Mind of the European Romantics* (1966).

Stang, R., *The Theory of the Novel in England, 1830–1870* (1959).

Thrall, M. M. H., *Rebellious Fraser's* (1934).

Watson, G., *The Literary Critics* (Penguin Books: 1962).

Watt, I., *The Rise of the Novel* (1957).

B. EDITIONS OF EMILY BRONTË'S WORKS

Poems by Currer, Ellis and Acton Bell (Aylott and Jones, 1846; reissued, Smith, Elder, 1848).

Wuthering Heights. A Novel, by Ellis Bell, with *Agnes Grey*, by Acton Bell, 3 vols (T. C. Newby, 1847).

Wuthering Heights and Agnes Grey, by Ellis and Acton Bell. *A new edition with a Biographical Notice of the authors, a selection from their literary remains, and a Preface by Currer Bell* (Smith, Elder, 1850).

The Complete Works of Emily Jane Brontë, ed. C. K. Shorter: vol. I: Poetry, with an Introductory Essay by W. Robertson Nicholl; vol. II: Prose, with an introduction by C. K. Shorter (1910–11). Some of the poems are incorrectly attributed.

The Complete Poems of Emily Jane Brontë, edited from the manuscripts, by C. W. Hatfield (Columbia University Press and Oxford University Press, 1941).

Five Essays Written in French by Emily Jane Brontë, ed. F. E. Ratchford, translations by L. Nagel (University of Texas, 1948).

Gondal Poems: now published from the manuscript in the British Museum, ed. H. Brown and J. Mott (Shakespeare Head Press, 1938).

Wuthering Heights. The Haworth Edition: Introduction by Mrs Humphry Ward (1899); Shakespeare Head (1931); 'World's Classics': Introduction by H. W. Garrod, ed. F. Page (1930); Everyman's Library (1955); Text, Sources, Criticism, ed. T. Moser (Harbrace Sourcebooks: 1962); An Authoritative Text, with essays in criticism, ed. W. M. Sale (Norton Critical Editions: 1963); Penguin English Library, ed. D. Daiches (1965); introduced by M. Schorer (Rinehart, 1950).

C. TEXTUAL AND BIBLIOGRAPHICAL STUDIES

Bentley, P., *The Brontë Sisters* (*British Book News* Supplement, 1950).

Blackburn, Ruth H., *The Brontë Sisters. Selected Source Materials* (1964).

Blondel, J., *Emily Brontë* (Presses Universitaires de France: 1955). (Bibliography.)

Christian, M. G., 'A Census of Brontë MSS in the United States', in *Trollopian*, Dec 1947 and March 1948. Supplement, vol. IV (1949).

—— 'The Brontës', in *Victorian Fiction, a guide to research*, ed. L. Stevenson (1964).

Cook, Davidson, 'The Honresfeld MS', in *Nineteenth Century and After*, C (Aug 1926).

Dean, C., 'Joseph's Speech in *Wuthering Heights*', in *NQ* CCV (Feb 1960).

Green, J. A., *Catalogue to the Gleave Brontë Collection, Moss Side Free Library* (Manchester, 1907).

Isenberg, D. M., 'A Gondal Fragment', in *BST* XIV, pt 72 (1962).

Jones, J. J., 'The Wise-Symington Papers' (a note on acquisition) in *Library Chronicle, University of Texas*, III (1950).

Lane, Margaret, 'Emily Jane Brontë's *Palace of Death* essay' (translation), in *BST* XII, pt 64 (1954).

Parrish, M. L., *Victorian Lady Novelists: First Editions in the Library of Dormy House, Pine Valley, New Jersey* (1933).

Ratchford, F. E., 'The Correct Text of Emily Jane Brontë's Poems', in *BST* X, pt 52 (1942) (review of the Hatfield edition).

—— (ed.) 'A Diary Paper by Emily Brontë', transcript and commentary, in *BST* XII, pt 61 (1951).

Ruff, W., 'First American Editions of the Brontë Novels', in *BST* VIII, pt 44 (1934).

Weir, E. M., 'The Complete Poems of Emily Brontë', in *BST* XII, pt 62 (1952) (review of the Henderson edition).

Wise, Thomas J., *A Bibliography of the Writings in Prose and Verse of the Brontë family*, with Supplement (1917).

Wood, Butler, 'A Bibliography of the Works of the Brontë Family', in *BST* I, pt 1 and 6 (1895, 1897).

'Three Essays by Emily Jane Brontë' (reprinted from Ratchford, *Five Essays in French*), in *BST* XI, pt 60 (1950).

Schmidt, E. T., 'Charlotte Brontë's Editorial Changes in Emily's Poems', in *BST* XV, pt 78 (1968).

D. BIOGRAPHICAL SOURCES AND STUDIES

Andrews, W. L., 'The Centenary of Emily Brontë's Death', in *BST* XI, pt 59 (1949).

Bentley, P., *The Brontës* (1947).

Bradby, G. F., *The Brontës and other Essays* (1937).

Chadwick, E. A., *In the Footsteps of the Brontës* (1914).

—— 'Emily Brontë as Lawyer', in *Bookman*, Nov 1926 (review of *The Structure of Wuthering Heights*, by 'C.P.S.').

Chapple, J. A. V., and Pollard, A. (ed.), *The Letters of Mrs Gaskell* (1966).

Charlier, Gustave, 'Brussels Life in Villette', in *BST* XII, pt 65 (1955).

Childe, W. R., 'The Literary Background of the Brontës', in *BST* X, pt 54 (1944).

Cornish, D. H., 'The Brontës' Study of French', in *BST* XI, pt 57 (1947).

Crowther, G., 'The Rev. P. Brontë's Tax Returns', in *BST* XII, pt 65 (1955).

Cunliffe, W. R., 'Emily Brontë, a Clue to her Appearance', in *BST* XIII, pt 69 (1959).

Curtis, Myra, 'Charlotte Brontë in her Letters', in *BST* XIII, pt 70 (1960).

—— 'Cowan Bridge', in *BST* XII, pt 63 (1950).

—— on the 'Profile' portrait, in *BST* XIII, pt 69 (1959).

Dimnet, the Abbé, *Les Sœurs Brontë* (1910).

Dingle, Herbert, 'An Examination of Emily Brontë's Poetry', in *BST* XIV, pt 74 (1964).

du Maurier, Daphne, *The Infernal World of Branwell Brontë* (1960).

Dupont, V., 'Trois Notes sur les Brontë', in *Études Anglaises*, no. 1, ann. 6 (1933) p. 16.

Edgerley, C. M., 'A National Portrait Vindicated', in *BST* VIII, pt 42 (1932). See also *BST* XIII, pt 68 (1958) and 69 (1959); *BST* V, pt 24 (1914).

—— 'Ponden Hall and the Heatons', in *BST* X, pt 55 (1945).

Edwards, R. A., 'The Brontës and Methodism', in *TLS* 3 June 1949 (correspondence). Also *TLS* 20 and 27 May 1949 (P. Bentley and T. Olsen).

Erskine Stuart, J. A., *The Brontë Country* (1888).

Field, W. T., 'Two Brussels Schoolfellows of the Brontës', in *BST* V, pt 23 (1913).

Gaskell, E. C., *The Life of Charlotte Brontë*, 2 vols (Smith, Elder: 1857). References in the notes are to the amended 3rd edition, with an introduction by C. K. Shorter ('World's Classics': 1919).

Gérin, Winifred, *Branwell Brontë* (1961).

—— *Anne Brontë* (1959).

—— *Charlotte Brontë* (1967).

Gleave, J. J., *Emily Brontë: an appreciation* (1904).

Green, J. J., 'The Brontë-Wheelwright Friendship', in *Friends' Quarterly Examiner*, L, no. 197–8 (1916). Draft letter, typescript, L. Wheelwright to Shorter, in BPM, item 571.

Grundy, F. H., *Pictures of the Past* (1879).

Hanson, L. and E. M., *The Four Brontës* (1949).

Hanson, T. W., 'The Local Colour of *Wuthering Heights*', in *BST* VI, pt 34 (1924).

Harrison, Ada, *Anne Brontë* (1959).

Harrison, G. E., *Haworth Parsonage: a study of Wesley and the Brontës* (Wesley Hist. Soc.: 1937).

—— *The Clue to the Brontës* (1948).

Hatfield, C. W., 'Emily Brontë's Lost Love', in *TLS* 29 Aug 1936.

Hawkes, Jacquetta, 'Emily Brontë in the Natural Scene', in *BST* XII, pt 63 (1953).

Hedley, A., 'Emily Brontë's Second Novel', in *TLS* 6 Sept 1947 (correspondence).

Hewish, J., 'Emily Brontë's Missing Novel', in *TLS* 10 March 1966 (correspondence); also *BST* XV, pt 76 (1966).

Hinkley, L., *The Brontës, Charlotte and Emily* (1947).

Hope Dodds, M., 'George Hudson and the Brontës', in *BST* XIV, pt 72 (1962).

Hopkins, Annette B., *The Father of the Brontës* (1958).

Hutton, J., 'Items From the Parsonage Press Cuttings Book', in *BST* XIV, pt 73 (1963).

Lane, Margaret, *The Brontë Story* (1953).

—— 'The Drug-like Brontë Dream', in *BST* XII, pt 62 (1952).

Law, Alice, *Emily Jane Brontë and the Authorship of Wuthering Heights* (1928).

Lemon, C., 'Sickness and Health in *Wuthering Heights*', in *BST* XIV, pt 73 (1963).

Leyland, F. A., *The Brontë Family*, 2 vols (1885, 1886).

Lock, J., and Dixon, A., *Man of Sorrow* (1965).

Loudan, Jack, 'The Brontës in Ulster', in *Listener*, 18 Dec 1952.

MacCarthy, Desmond, 'The Brontës in their Books', in *BST* X, pt 55 (1945).

Macdonald, Frederika, *The Secret of Charlotte Brontë* (1914).

Marsden, Hilda, 'The Scenic Background of *Wuthering Heights*', in *BST* XIII,

'The Miraculous Parsonage', in *TLS* 17 July 1948 (review of P. Henderson, *Poems*, and L. Hinkley, *The Brontës, Charlotte and Emily*).

Nixon, Ingeborg, 'The Brontë Portraits', in *BST* XIII, pt 68 (1958).

Nussey, E., 'Reminiscences of Charlotte Brontë', in *Scribner's Monthly*, May 1871 ; also *BST* II, pt 10 (1899).

Ratchford, F. E., *The Brontës' Web of Childhood* (1941).

Raymond, E., *In the Steps of the Brontës* (1948).

—— 'The Brontë Legend: its cause and treatment', in *Essays by Divers Hands*, XXVI (1953).

Reid, Wemyss, *Memoirs* (1905) ch. x.

Robinson, A. M. F., *Emily Brontë* (1883).

Scott, R. M., 'High Sunderland Hall in Decay', in *BST* XI, pt 59 (1949).

Scruton, W., *Thornton and the Brontës* (1898).

Shorter, C. K., *Charlotte Brontë and Her Circle* (1896); *The Brontës and their Circle* (a reissue: 1914).

Shorter, C. K., *The Brontës, Life and Letters* (1908).

Simpson, Charles, *Emily Brontë* (1929).

Sinclair, May, *The Three Brontës* (1912).

Smith, George, 'The Brontës', in *Cornhill*, July 1873.

Snowden, K., 'The Enigma of Emily Brontë', in *Fortnightly Review*, Aug 1928.

Spark, Muriel, and Stanford, D., *Emily Brontë* (1953).

Spielman, M. H., *The Brontë-Heger Letters* (1919); also *BST* v, pt 24 (1914).

Steen, E., 'Problemet Emily Brontë', in *Edda*, XLIX (1949).

Symons, Arthur, *Dramatis Personae* (1923) pp. 44–53.

Thorburn, D. B., 'The Effects of the Wesleyan Movement on the Brontë Sisters' (thesis), New York, 1948).

Thackeray, Anne Isabella, *Chapters from some Memories* (1894).

Timings, E. K., 'A Great Fancy for Arms', in *BST* XIV, pt 71 (1961).

Weir, E. M., 'A Picture Attributed to Emily Brontë', in *BST* XI, pt 59 (1949).

—— 'Cowan Bridge: new light from old documents', in *BST* XI, pt 56 (1946).

Whone, Clifford, 'Where the Brontës Borrowed Books', in *BST* XI, pt 60 (1950).

Williams, A. M., 'Emily Brontë', in *Temple Bar Magazine*, XCVIII (1893) 431.

Willis, Irene C., *The Authorship of Wuthering Heights* (1936).

—— *The Brontës* (1933; Duckworth Paperback, 1957).

Wilson, W. Romer, *All Alone* (1928).

Wise, Thomas J., and Symington, J. A., The Shakespeare Head Brontë, 19 vols (Blackwell, 1931–8).

Wright, W., *The Brontës in Ireland* (1893).

Yates, W. W., *The Father of the Brontës* (1897).

E. CRITICISM

Adams, R. M., '*Wuthering Heights*, Land East of Eden', in *NCF* XIII (June 1958).

Allen, Walter, *The English Novel* (Penguin: 1958), pp. 194–8.

Allott, Miriam, in *EC* no. 2 (1959) (review of Mary Visick, *The Genesis of Wuthering Heights*).

—— 'The Rejection of Heathcliff', in *EC* VIII, no. 1 (1958).

Baker, E. A., *The History of the English Novel* (1924–39) VIII, ch. II, pp. 64–7.

Bald, M. A., *Women Novelists of the Nineteenth Century* (1923).

Bataille, G., 'Emily Brontë', in *La Littérature et le Mal* (Paris, 1957).

Bell, Vereen M., '*Wuthering Heights* and the Unforgivable Sin', in *NCF* XVII (Sept 1962).

Bentley, P., on the daydream writings, in *Listener*, 27 Jan 1949.

Blondel, J., *Emily Brontë: expérience spirituelle et création poétique* (Clermont, and Presses Universitaires de France: 1955).

—— 'Nouveaux Regards sur Emily Brontë' (reviews), in *Annales de Faculté de Lettres d'Aix*, XXXV (1961).

Blondel, J., 'Cent Ans de critique autour d'Emily Brontë' in *Les Langues Modernes*, ann. XLII (1948).

—— in *Études Anglaises*, VIII, ann. 3 (1955) (review of M. Spark and D. Stanford, *Emily Brontë*).

Bloomfield, L., '*Wuthering Heights*', in *Time and Tide*, 20 March 1948.

Booth, Bradford Allen, 'Form and Technique in the Novel', in *The Reinterpretation of Victorian Literature*, ed. J. E. Baker (1950).

Bradby, G. F., 'Emily Brontë', in *Nineteenth Century*, CVIII (Oct 1930) 533.

Bradner, L., 'The Growth of *Wuthering Heights*', in *PMLA* XLVIII (March 1933).

Brick, A. R., 'Lewes' Review of *Wuthering Heights*', in *NCF* XIV (March 1960).

—— in *NCF* XIII (March 1959) (review of Mary Visick, *The Genesis of Wuthering Heights*).

Brown, H., 'The Influence of Byron on Emily Brontë', in *MLR* XXXIV (1939).

Buchen, I. H., 'Emily Brontë and the Metaphysics of Childhood', in *NCF* XXI (June 1967).

Buckler, W. E., 'Chapter VII of *Wuthering Heights*, a Key', in *NCF* VII (June 1952).

Cecil, David, 'Emily Brontë and *Wuthering Heights*', in *Early Victorian Novelists* (1934).

Chase, R., 'The Brontës: a centennial observance', in *KR* IX, no. 4 (autumn 1947) 487. Reprinted in *Forms of Modern Fiction*, ed. Van O'Connor (1948).

Chesterton, G. K., in *The Victorian Age in Literature* (1913).

Clay, C. T., 'Notes on the Chronology of *Wuthering Heights*', in *BST* XII, pt 62 (1952).

Collins, Clifford, 'Theme and Convention in *Wuthering Heights*', in *Critic*, 1947.

Cooper, D. J., 'A French Thesis on Emily Brontë', a summary in *BST* XII, pt 64 (1954).

—— 'The Romantics and Emily Brontë', in *BST* XII, pt 62 (1952).

Daiches, D., in *A Critical History of English Literature* (1960) II.

—— in *New Republic*, 25 Sept 1950 (review of L. and E. M. Hanson, *The Four Brontës*).

Davis, R. G. 'The Sense of the Real in English Fiction', in *Comparative Literature*, III (1951).

De Villiers, J., '*Wuthering Heights*', in *Standpunte*, XI (1956-7).

Dobrée, Bonamy, Introduction to *Wuthering Heights* (Collins: 1954).

Dohm, H., 'Die Technik der Charakter Darstellung . . . im *Wuthering Heights*' (thesis, Innsbruck, 1955).

Drew, Arnold P., 'Emily Brontë and Hamlet', in *NQ* CIC (Feb 1954) 81.

Drew, P., 'Charlotte Brontë as Critic of *Wuthering Heights*', in *NCF* XVIII (March 1964).

Dry, F. S., *The Sources of Wuthering Heights* (Brontë Sources no. 1: 1937).

Dugas, J. H., 'The Literary Reputation of the Brontës, 1846-1951' (thesis, University of Illinois), abstract in *DA* XII (1952).

Durrell, L., quoted in 'Dylan Thomas and Emily Brontë', in *BST* XIV, pt 73 (1963).

Escombe, Lucien, *Emily Brontë et ses démons* (Paris, 1941).

Ewbank, Inga-Stina, *Their Proper Sphere* (1966).

Fenton, E. M., 'The Spirit of *Wuthering Heights* as distinguished from that of Gothic romance', in *Washington University Studies*, VIII (Humanistic Series, no. 1: St Louis, Mo. 1920).

Ford, Boris, '*Wuthering Heights*', in *Scrutiny*, March 1939.

Ford, Ford Madox, *The English Novel* (1930) p. 108.

Fraser, H., 'The Name of Action', in *NCF* XX (Dec 1965).

Froese, F., 'Untersuchungen zu Emily Brontës Roman' (dissertation, Königsberg, 1920). Abstract in *Inaug. Diss. d. Phil. Fak. Königsberg*, i PS 135–8, by 'Steinbacher'.

Gettmann, Royal A., Introduction to *Wuthering Heights* (New York Modern Library: 1950).

Girdler, L., '*Wuthering Heights* and Shakespeare', in *Huntington Library Quarterly*, XIX (Aug 1956).

Goldstone, H., '*Wuthering Heights* Revisited', in *English Journal*, XLVIII (April 1959).

Goodridge, J. F., *Wuthering Heights* (Studies in English Literature, no. 20: Arnold, 1964).

Gose, Elliott B., '*Wuthering Heights*, the Heath and the Hearth', in *NCF* XXI (June 1966).

Gosse, Edmund, 'The Challenge of the Brontës', in *Some Diversions of a Man of Letters* (1905).

Haflèy, James, 'The Villain in *Wuthering Heights*', in *NCF* XIII (June 1958).

Hannah, B., *The Brontës* (Guild of Pastoral Psychology Lecture 68: 1950).

Holloway, Owen E., '*Wuthering Heights*: a matter of method', in *Northern Miscellany*, no. 1 (autumn 1953).

Insh, G. P., 'Haworth Pilgrimage', in *BST* X, pt 54 (1944).

Jaloux, E., 'Le Mystère d'Emily Brontë', in *D'Eschyle à Giraudoux* (1946).

Jordan, J. E., 'The Ironic Vision of Emily Brontë', in *NCF* XX (June 1965).

Justus, J., 'Beyond Gothicism: *Wuthering Heights* and an American tradition', in *Tennessee Studies in Literature*, V (1960).

Kavanagh, C., *The Symbolism of Wuthering Heights* (1920).

Kettle, Arnold, *The English Novel* (1951).

Klingopulos, G. D., '*Wuthering Heights*' (The Novel as Dramatic Poem), in *Scrutiny*, XIV, no. 4 (1947).

—— in *Études Anglaises*, 1956 (review of J. Blondel, *Emily Brontë*).

—— in *The Pelican Guide to English Literature*, VI 95–6 (the poems).

Kuhlman, R., *Der Naturpaganismus in der Weltanschauung von Emily Brontë* (dissertation, Bonn, 1927).

Langman, K., '*Wuthering Heights*', in *Approaches to the Novel*, ed. J. Colmer (1967).

Leavis, F. R., 'The Brontës', a note in *The Great Tradition* (1948) p. 27.

Lehman, B. H., '*Wuthering Heights*', in *English Studies*, 1955.

Lettis, R., and Morris, W. E., *A Wuthering Heights Handbook* (Odyssey Press: New York, 1961).

Lewis, C. Day, 'Emily Brontë', in *Notable Images of Virtue* (1954); also in *BST* XIII, pt 67 (1957).

Livermore, Anne L., 'Byron and Emily Brontë', in *Quarterly Review*, 1962.

Lucas, P. D., *An Introduction to the Psychology of Wuthering Heights* (Guild of Pastoral Psychology: 1943).

MacCarthy, B. G., 'Emily Brontë', in *Studies, an Irish Quarterly*, XXXIX (March 1950).

McCullough, B. G., *Representative English Novelists* (New York, 1946), ch. 12, 'The Dramatic Novel'.

McKibben, R. C., 'The Image of the Book in *Wuthering Heights*', in *NCF* XV (Sept 1960).

Maeterlinck, Maurice, in *Wisdom and Destiny* (1898).

Marshall, W. H., 'Hareton Earnshaw. Natural Theology on the Moors', in *Victorian Newsletter* (1962).

Mathison, J. K., 'Nelly Dean and the Power of *Wuthering Heights*', in *NCF* XV (Sept 1960).

Maugham, W. Somerset, 'Emily Brontë and *Wuthering Heights*', in *Ten Novels and their Authors* (1954).

Mayne, Isobel, 'Emily Brontë's Mr Lockwood', in *BST* XV, pt 78 (1968).

Maxwell, J. C., 'Emily Brontë's Palace of Death', in *BST* XV, pt 77 (1967).

Miller, J. H., 'Emily Brontë', in *The Disappearance of God* (1963).

'The Miraculous Parsonage', in *TLS* 17 July 1948 (reviews of L. Hinkley, *The Brontës, Charlotte and Emily*, and P. Henderson, *Emily Brontë. Selected Poems.*

Moody, P., 'The Challenge to Maturity in *Wuthering Heights*', in *Melbourne Critical Review*, no. 5 (1962).

Moser, Thomas, 'What is the Matter with Emily Jane?' in *NCF* XVII (June 1962).

Muir, Edwin, in *Observer*, 19 Dec 1948.

Nelson, Jane Grey, 'First American Reviews of the Works of the Brontës', in *BST* XIV, pt 74 (1964).

Odom, K. C., 'The Brontës and Romantic Views of Personality' (thesis, Wisconsin University), abstract in *DA* 1961.

Pritchett, V. S., in *New Statesman*, 22 June 1946.

Ralli, Augustus, 'Emily Brontë: the problem of personality', in *North American Review*, CCXXI (March 1925) 495.

Ratchford, F. E., 'War in Gondal', in *Trollopian*, II (1947).

—— 'Letters from a Brontë Cousin' (i.e. E. J. Kingston), correspondence in *TLS* 11 Dec 1948.

Ray, G. N., in *Review of English Studies*, NS II (1950–1) (review of L. and E. M. Hanson, *The Four Brontës*).

Read, Herbert, 'Charlotte and Emily Brontë', in *Yale Review*, July 1925. Reprinted in *Reason and Romanticism*, 1926.

S[anger], C. P., *The Structure of Wuthering Heights* (1926).

Schermbach, V., 'Naturdarstellung und Naturempfindung bei den Brontës' (thesis, Munster, 1931).

Schorer, M., 'Fiction and the Matrix of Analogy', in *KR* XI (autumn 1949); reprinted in *Critiques and Essays on Modern Fiction, 1920–51*, ed. J. W. Aldridge (1951).

Shannon, Edgar F., Jr., 'Lockwood's Dreams and the Exegesis of *Wuthering Heights*', in *NCF* XIV (Sept 1959).

Simon, Irene, *Formes du roman anglais de Dickens à Joyce* (Liège, 1949).

Smith, J. C., 'Emily Brontë, A Reconsideration', in *ES* V (1914).

Solomon, E., 'The Incest Theme in *Wuthering Heights*', in *NCF* XIV (June 1959).

Spens, Janet, 'Charlotte Brontë', in *ES* XIV (1929).

Spark, M., and Stanford, D., *Emily Brontë: her life and work* (1953).

Tillotson, Kathleen, *Novels of the Eighteen-Forties* (1954).

—— in *MLR* XLV (1950) 536–40 (on L. and E. M. Hanson's *The Four Brontës*).

Traversi, Derek, 'The Brontë Sisters and *Wuthering Heights*', in *The Pelican Guide to English Literature*, VI (1958) 256–72.

—— '*Wuthering Heights* after 100 Years', in *Dublin Review*, no 445 (Spring 1949).

Turnell, Martin, 'Style in *Wuthering Heights*', in *Dublin Review*, CCVI (Jan–March 1940).

Van Ghent, D., 'The Window Figure and the Two Children Figure in *Wuthering Heights*', in *NCF* VII (Dec 1952); reprinted in *The English Novel, Form and Function* (1953).

Visick, Mary, *The Genesis of Wuthering Heights* (1958).

Wain, John, 'Pseudo-classic? No', in *Observer*, 16 March 1958.

Ward, Mrs Humphry, Introduction to *Wuthering Heights*, Haworth Edition (1899–1900). Also '*Wuthering Heights*', in *BST* II, pt 15 (1906).

Watkins, J. B. C., 'The Brontë Myth', in *Canadian Forum*, XII (1932).

Watson, M. R., 'Tempest in the Soul! The Theme and Structure of *Wuthering Heights*', in *NCF* IV (Sept 1949).

—— '*Wuthering Heights* and the Critics', in *Trollopian*, III (1948).

Wilson, D., 'Emily Brontë, First of the Moderns', in *Modern Quarterly Miscellany*, no.1 (1947).

Woodring, C., 'The Narrators of *Wuthering Heights*', in *NCF* XII (March 1957).

Woolf, Virginia, '*Jane Eyre* and *Wuthering Heights*', in (First) *Common Reader* (1925) p. 196.

Zaandvoort, R. W., 'Recent Literature on the Brontës', in *English Studies* (Amsterdam, Dec 1943).

F. STUDIES OF THE POEMS

Bridges, Robert, in *Collected Essays*, IX (1932).

Brown, H., and Mott, J., 'The Gondal Saga', in *BST* IX, pt 48 (1938).

Carr, D. R. W., 'The Sphinx of English Poetry', in *Poetry Review*, XXXIV (1943) 85.

Dobson, M., 'Was Emily Brontë a Mystic?' in *BST* XI, pt 58 (1948).

Dodds, M. H., in *MLR* XXXVIII (1943) 154 (review of C. W. Hatfield, *Complete Poems*).

—— 'Gondaliand', in *MLR* XVIII (1923).

—— 'A Second Visit to Gondaliand', in *MLR* XXI (1926).

—— 'Heathcliff's Country', in *MLR* XXXIX (1944).

Evans, M., 'Byron and Emily Brontë', in *Life and Letters*, LVII (June 1948).

Garnett, R. (ed.), a selection of poems, in A. H. Miles, *Poets and Poetry of the Century* (1891).

Grierson, H. J. C., and Smith, J. C., *A Critical History of English Poetry* (1944) pp. 426–7.

Henderson, P. (ed.), *The Complete Poems of Emily Jane Brontë* (1951).

—— (ed.), *Poems by Emily Brontë* (1947).

Jack, A. A., *The Cambridge History of English Literature*, XIII 412 ff.

Laski, Marghanita, *Ecstasy* (Cresset Press, 1961) esp. pp. 47–54, 175.

Leavis, F. R., 'Reality and Sincerity. An Exercise in Critical Comparison', in *Scrutiny*, XIX (winter 1952/3).

Mackay, A. M., 'On the Interpretation of Emily Brontë', in *Westminster Review*, CL (Aug 1898).

Maurer, K. W., 'The Poetry of Emily Brontë', in *Anglia*, XLIX (June 1937).

Morgan, E., 'Women and Poetry', in *Cambridge Journal*, III (1950) 648.

—— 'Emily Brontë's Poems', in *TLS* 12 Feb 1949 (correspondence).

Paden, W. D., *An Investigation of Gondal* (*Bookman* Monograph: New York, 1958).

Raine, Kathleen, in *New Statesman*, 8 March 1952.

Ratchford, F. E., *Gondal's Queen* (1955).

—— 'War in Gondal', in *Trollopian*, II (1947).

Sonnino, Gorgina, 'Il Pensiero Religioso di una Poetessa Inglese', in *Nuova Antologia*, quarta serie, Jan–Feb 1904 (Rome).

Spark, M. (ed.), *A Selection of Poems by Emily Jane Brontë* (1952).

Spurgeon, C., *Mysticism in English Literature* (1913). (The Cambridge Manuals of Science and Literature.)

Symons, A. (ed.), *Poems of Emily Brontë* (1906).

Visick, Mary, in *NCF* XIV (June 1959) (review of W. D. Paden, *An Investigation of Gondal*).

Weir, E. M., in *BST* XII, pt 62 (1952) (review of P. Henderson, *Complete Poems*).

Willy, M., 'Emily Brontë, Poet and Mystic', in *English*, VI (1946).

TLS 29 Jan 1949 (a review of P. Henderson, selected *Poems* by EB).

Anon. *NQ* CLXXXVI (17 June 1944) 281 (EB's poems).

Anon. *NQ* CLI (1926) 127 (the 'Honresfeld' manuscript).

G. NINETEENTH-CENTURY REVIEWS

Athenaeum, 4 July 1846, p. 682 ('Poetry of the Million').

Critic, 4 July 1846, p. 6.

Dublin University Magazine, xxviii (Oct 1846) ('Evenings with our Younger Poets', by [William Archer] B[utler]).

Athenaeum, 25 Dec 1847; 28 Dec 1850 (the latter is a review of the 2nd edition of *Wuthering Heights*).

Examiner, 8 Jan 1848; 21 Dec 1850 (2nd edition of *Wuthering Heights*).

Britannia, 15 Jan 1848, pp. 42–3 (*Wuthering Heights*).

Douglas Jerrold's Weekly Newspaper, 15 Jan 1848 (*Wuthering Heights*).

Atlas, 22 Jan 1848 (*Wuthering Heights*).

Economist, 29 Jan 1848, p. 126; 4 Jan 1851, p. 15 (the latter reviews the 2nd edition of *Wuthering Heights*).

Tait's Edinburgh Magazine, xv (Feb 1848) (*Wuthering Heights*).

Peterson's Magazine, March 1848 (the *Poems* and *Wuthering Heights*; see Jane Grey Nelson, 'First American Reviews of the Works of the Brontës', in *BST* xiv, pt 74 (1964).

Literary World, April 1848 (*Wuthering Heights*; see Nelson, op. cit.).

American Review, June 1848, pp. 571–2 (G. W. Peck on *Wuthering Heights*; see Nelson, op. cit.).

Graham's Magazine, July 1848 (*Wuthering Heights*; see Nelson, op. cit.).

North American Review, Oct 1848 (E. P. Whipple on *Wuthering Heights*); Oct 1857 (on the works of the Brontës). (See Nelson, op. cit.)

Spectator, 4 Nov 1848, pp. 1094–5 (a review of the Smith, Elder reissue of *Poems*).

Critic, no. 185 (15 Dec 1848) ('Cento of Poetry': on the reissued *Poems*).

Literary Gazette, 30 Dec 1848 (another review of the reissued *Poems*).

Quarterly Review, lxxxiv (Dec 1848; March 1849) (Lady E. Eastlake on *Jane Eyre*; *Wuthering Heights* is referred to).

Palladium, Sept 1850 (Sydney Dobell on Charlotte Brontë's novels and on *Wuthering Heights*). Reprinted in *Life and Letters of S. Dobell*, i (1878) 168 ff.

Leader, 28 Dec 1850 (G. H. Lewes on the 2nd edition of *Wuthering Heights*).

Review of *Wuthering Heights*, source unknown, probably 1848. Reprinted in C. Simpson, *Emily Brontë* (1929).

W.P.P., *Jottings on Currer, Ellis and Acton Bell* (1856).

Fraser's Magazine, lv (May 1857), 'Charlotte Brontë' (John Skelton); also lx (July 1859) 'Thoughts on Modern English Literature' (V. H. Hobart). Reprinted in *Fragments* (1875); *Essays and Miscellaneous Writings* (1885). (Both pieces discuss *Wuthering Heights*.)

National Review, v (July 1857), 'Miss Brontë' (W. C. Roscoe). Reprinted in *Essays*, ii (1860) (*Wuthering Heights* and *Poems*).

Blackwood's Magazine, July 1857, 'Currer Bell' (Eneas Sweetland Dallas on Charlotte Brontë, with extensive reference to Emily Brontë).

Bayne, Peter, 'Ellis, Acton and Currer Bell', in *Essays in Biography and Criticism*, 1st Series (Boston, 1857). Also *Two Great English Women* (1871).

Cornhill, XXXVI (Dec 1877), 'Hours in a Library, no. 17. Charlotte Brontë' (Leslie Stephen; with references to Emily Brontë and *Wuthering Heights*).

Athenaeum, 16 June 1883 (a review of A. M. F. Robinson, *Emily Brontë* (A. C. Swinburne)).

BST II, pt 9 (1898), 'The Position of the Brontës as Origins . . .' (G. Saintsbury).

Notes

Note. See p. 173 for List of Abbreviations.

INTRODUCTION: THE SOURCES (pages 13–20)

1. EB to EN, May 1843(?), BM Ashley MS 177; SHB I 298.
2. CB to WSW, 3 Jan 1850; SHB III 63.
3. *Scribner's Monthly*, May 1871; *BST* II, pt 10.
4. Quoted by S. Biddell, SHB IV 278.
5. Gaskell to ?; Chapple and Pollard (ed.), *Letters of Mrs Gaskell*, no. 167, p. 249.
6. *Scribner's Monthly*, May 1871.
7. *Life*, ch. VIII.
8. *Jane Eyre*, ch. XXVIII.
9. CB to EN, 21 Dec 1839; SHB I 193.
10. CB to EN, Sept 1850; SHB III 166.
11. CB to WSW, 16 Nov 1848; SHB II 271.
12. Biographical Notice of Ellis and Acton Bell, 1850.
13. Gaskell to ?; Chapple and Pollard (ed.), *Letters of Mrs Gaskell*, no. 166, p. 247.
14. Gaskell to E. Shaen; Chapple and Pollard (ed.), *Letters of Mrs Gaskell*, no. 308, p. 409.
15. Shorter, *The Brontës and their Circle*, 'Preliminary'.
16. *Life*, ch. V.
17. CB to EN, 24 March 1845(?); SHB II 28.

BOOK ONE: I (pages 23–31)

1. 'Papa would like to see the work very much' (W. Carus, *The Memoirs of the Life of Charles Simeon*) 'as he knew Mr Simeon.' CB to EN, 3 May 1848; SHB II 212; also J. H. Buckley, *Tennyson* (1960) pp. 25–6.
2. *The Way of All Flesh*, ch. XLVII, etc.
3. Oram, in *BST* XIV, pt 74; Hatfield, in *BST* IX, pt 49.
4. Harrison, *The Clue to the Brontës*, ch. VI; also *BST*, various contributions on Miss Branwell.

5. *The Professor*, ch. VII.

6. CB to Gaskell, 9 July 1853; SHB IV 76.

7. PB to Mrs Franks, 6 July 1835; SHB I 130.

8. A. M. Mackay, quoted SHB I 70–3.

9. Lock and Dixon, *A Man of Sorrow*, p. 235.

10. *The Way of All Flesh*, ch. XXIV.

11. PB to Mrs Franks, 13 June 1836; SHB I 144.

12. Mesmerism in Haworth, in *Bradford Observer*, 27 April 1843; E. K. Timings, in *BST* XIV, pt 71.

13. Letter, PB to Mrs Gaskell, 30 July 1855 (now in Christie Library, Manchester University); *BST* IX, pts 43, 44.

14. Gaskell to R. S. Oldham, 1 June 1858. Chapple and Pollard (ed.), *Letters of Mrs Gaskell*, no. 347A, p. 448.

15. EN in *Scribner's Monthly*, May 1871.

16. Gérin, *Charlotte Brontë*, pp. 41 ff.

17. Reproductions, BPM Collection; vignettes from T. Bewick, *Birds* (1805 ed.) II 213, or (1809 ed.) p. 252 (M. G. Christian's catalogue no. 1012); engraving, Weir, in *BST* XI, pt 59.

18. Hayter, *Mrs Browning*, p. 13.

19. *Life*, ch. V.

20. 'Tales of the Islanders', quoted in *Life*, ch. V.

21. *Life*, ch. V.

22. Gérin, *Branwell Brontë*, p. 31.

23. Mary Taylor to Gaskell, 18 Jan 1856; SHB I 91.

24. 'Rogue in Public', in 'Monthly Intelligencer', 27 March 1833; SHBMU I 183; 'A Complaint by Rogue', p. 195 ('rival GENII THRONES').

25. Christian, 'Census of Brontë MSS' in *Trollopian*, IV (1948) 245.

26. 'The Foundling' ('Chapter the IX'); SHBMU I 275.

27. *Life*, ch. V, 'Tales of the Islanders'; 'Emily [chose] Walter Scott . . .'

28. Paden, *An Investigation of Gondal*, p. 56.

29. Miller, *The Disappearance of God*, pp. 160–1.

BOOK ONE: II (pages 32–45)

1. CB to EN, 21 July 1832; SHB I 103.

2. EN in *Scribner's Monthly*, May 1871.

3. Portrait controversy: Edgerley, Nixon, Curtis, etc., in *BST* V, VIII, XIII.

4. CB to EN, 12 June 1850; SHB III 118; also W. R. Cunliffe, in *BST* XIII, pt 69.

5. *Shirley*, ch. XI.

6. Gaskell to ?; Chapple and Pollard (ed.), *Letters of Mrs Gaskell*, no. 167, p. 249.

7. CB to EN, July 1834, SHB I 121–2.

8. Shackleton, 'Four Hundred Years of a W. Yorkshire Family' (typescript, BPM).
9. Gérin, *Branwell Brontë*.
10. CB to De Quincey, 16 June 1847; SHB II 136.
11. *Pelican Guide*, V 140.
12. CB to EN, 2 July 1835; SHB I 129.
13. Diary paper, Bonnell Collection, BPM.
14. 'Extract from a diary of Lord Byron', quoted in *Works and Life*, by T. Moore (1832).
15. 'Preface to the Literary Remains', 1850.
16. Keighley Library Catalogue, 1841; *BST* XI, pt 60.
17. Henderson, *Poems by Emily Brontë* (selected).
18. Note, BPM Collection.
19. 'Memoir of the Early Life of Cowper', in *Poems*, ed. J. Johnson (1815).
20. *Life*, ch. VIII.

BOOK ONE: III (pages 46–71)

1. CB to EN, 2(?) Oct 1837; SHB I 162.
2. CB to EN, 9 June 1838; SHB I 167.
3. Chadwick, *In the Footsteps of the Brontës*, pp. 123–4.
4. Diary of Caroline Wyvile Walker, quoted by J. Lister, in *Halifax Antiquarian Society Papers* (1908) pp. 209–20; also Hanson, in *BST* VI, pt 34.
5. 1841 Census returns, Public Record Office.
6. *Halifax Guardian*, Dec 1842.
7. Chadwick, loc. cit.
8. Chadwick, p. 128.
9. *Far from the Madding Crowd*, Preface.
10. Lister, in *Halifax A.S. Papers*, loc. cit.; also Hanson, in *BST* VI, pt 34; Marsden, in *BST* XIII, pt 67.
11. Marsden, loc. cit.
12. Dingle, in *BST* XIV, pt 74.
13. *Old Mortality*, ch. XLIII.
14. CB to EB, 8 June 1839; *BST* I 178.
15. Birthday note, originally in Law Collection; transcript SHB I 239.
16. CB to EN, June 1840; SHB I 209.
17. Birthday note; transcript SHB II 51 (my emendation); SHB gives 'the'.
18. Shorter, *The Brontës and their Circle*, 'Preliminary'.
19. Birthday note; transcript SHB II 51.
20. CB to EN, 2 Nov 1841; CB to EB, 7 Nov 1841; SHB I 245–7.
21. 'Preface to Literary Remains', 1850.
22. *Charlotte Brontë*, ch. XIII and XIV.

23. CB to EN, May 1842; SHB I 260–1.
24. Weir, in *BST* XI, pt 59.
25. L. Quievreux, *Bruxelles, Les Brontës* (Brussels, Liège, 1953); also, Heger obituary, in *L'Indépendance Belge*, May 1896. Quoted in Chadwick, *In the Footsteps of the Brontës*, and Gérin, *Charlotte Brontë*, ch. XIII.
26. Frederika Macdonald, *The Secret of Charlotte Brontë*, p. 221.
27. *Life*, ch. XI; also Quievreux, op. cit.; *L'Indépendance Belge*, May 1896.
28. Heger Prospectus; SHB I 252.
29. *Villette*, ch. XXVIII.
30. L. Wheelwright to Shorter (draft letter), quoted J. J. Green, 'The Brontë-Wheelwright Friendship', typescript at BPM, item 571; also in *Friends' Quarterly Examiner*, L, no. 197–8 (1916).
31. Suggested in Miller, *The Disappearance of God*, p. 163 n.
32. Berg Collection, New York Public Library. Author's translation.
33. *Life*, ch. XI.
34. *Life*, ch. XI.
35. Bonnell Collection at BPM. Author's translation.
36. Berg Collection.
37. CB to EN, July 1842; SHB I 267.
38. Draft letter (see note 30).
39. Bassompierre to ?; transcript in *BST* 1913 (W. T. Field).
40. Maxwell, in *BST* XV, pt 77.
41. *Life*, ch. XI.
42. Mary Taylor to EN, 30 Oct 1842, postscript; SHB I 274–5. Mary Taylor to EN, 6 Feb 1843; SHB I 292.
43. Heger to PB, 5 Nov 1842; SHB I 279.

BOOK ONE: IV (pages 72–86)

1. CB to M. Wooler, 23 April 1845; SHB II 32.
2. Biographical Notice, 1850.
3. CB to EB, 2 Sept 1843; SHB I 303.
4. EB to EN, endorsed 'May 1843', BM Ashley MS 177; SHB I 298.
5. Birthday note; original in Law Collection; transcript SHB II 49–50.
6. BM Ashley MS 175.
7. CB to EN, 24 June 1845; SHB II 41.
8. Note; original in Law Collection; transcript, SHB II 49–50.
9. EB to EN, 18 July 1845?; BPM collection; SHB II 41; also in *BST* XII, pt 63. (The date is almost illegible on the MS.)
10. *Two Great English Women* (1881).
11. F. R. Leavis, in *Scrutiny*, XIX (1952/3).
12. Visick, *The Genesis of Wuthering Heights*, pp. 20–36.
13. *The Tragical History of Doctor Faustus*.

14. Wedemeyer, in *Persona*, 1949. *Psychological Abstracts*, 1950 (H. P. David).
15. H. Fingarette, 'The Ego and Mystic Selflessness', in *Psychoanalytical Review*, 1958. *Psychological Abstracts*, 1959 (D. Prager).

BOOK ONE: V (pages 87–105)

1. Biographical Notice, 1850.
2. *The Disappearance of God*, p. 162.
3. CB to EN, 7 Oct 1845; SHB II 62.
4. *Sämtliche Werke*, vol. XIII, ch. 16; quoted by Isaiah Berlin, in *Aspects of the Eighteenth Century*, ed. Earl Wasserman (Baltimore, 1965).
5. *Railway Times*, 27 Sept 1845.
6. Account-book, BPM collection; Christian cat. 1400 e (or c).
7. CB to M. Wooler, 30 Jan 1846; SHB II 76.
8. *Globe*, 27 April 1846.
9. CB to M. Wooler, 30 Jan 1846; SHB II 76.
10. EB to EN, 25 Feb 1846; SHB II 78.
11. CB to Aylott, 6 April 1846; SHB II 87.
12. 'A Census of Brontë MSS', in *Trollopian*, III (Dec 1947) 198.
13. CB to Henry Colburn, 4 July 1846; SHB IV 315.
14. *Life*, ch. xv.
15. *Novels of the Eighteen-Forties*, p. 282 n.
16. *Life*, ch. xv.
17. CB to EN; SHB II 105.
18. CB to EN, 24 July 1846; SHB II 105.
19. CB to EN, 14 May 1847; SHB II 133.
20. Chartists: CB to WSW, 25 Feb 1848, 11 March 1848; SHB II 190 ff.
21. *Life*, ch. xvi.
22. F. Boase, *Modern English Biography* (Truro, 1892–1908).
23. Sadleir, *Bibl. Soc. Trans.* 1924–5, pp. 218–19.
24. Sadleir, *XIXth Century Fiction. A bibliographical record based on his own collection* (1951).
25. CB to G. Smith, 18 Sept 1850; SHB III 160.
26. Trollope, *Autobiography* (Collins Fontana) p. 74; *Letters* (1951) pp. 4–5.
27. Trollope, *Autobiography*, p. 74.
28. CB to G. Smith, 7 Jan 1851; SHB III 196.
29. CB to WSW, 14 Dec 1847; SHB II 162.
30. CB to EN, 25 Sept 1847; SHB II 143.
31. AB to EN, 4 Oct 1847; SHB II 144.
32. Bonnell Collection, BPM; Simpson, *Emily Brontë*, pp. 167 ff.
33. CB to WSW, 15 Feb 1848; SHB II 189.
34. CB to WSW, 31 July 1848; SHB II 241.
35. Bonnell Collection, BPM; catalogue (1932) item I.

36. Second novel? See also *BST* xv, pt 76.
37. CB to EN, 29 Oct 1848; SHB II 268.
38. CB to WSW, 2 Nov 1848; SHB II 269.
39. CB to Dr Epps, 9 Dec 1848; SHB II 292n.
40. CB to WSW, 2 Nov 1848; SHB II 269.
41. CB to WSW, 22 Nov 1848; SHB II 286.
42. CB to WSW, 22 Nov 1848; SHB II 286.
43. CB to WSW, 22 Nov 1848; SHB II 286.
44. CB to EN, 23 Nov 1848; SHB II 288.
45. CB to WSW, 7 Dec 1848; SHB II 289. CB to WSW, 9 Dec; SHB II 291.
46. CB to Epps, 9 Dec 1848; SHB II 291.
47. *Life*, ch. XVI.
48. *Life*, ch. XVI.
49. CB to EN, 23 Nov 1848; SHB II 288.
50. *Life*, ch. XVI.
51. CB to WSW, 25 June 1849; SHB II 348.
52. CB to EN, 4 March 1852; SHB II 348.
53. CB to WSW, 25 June 1849; SHB II 350.
54. CB to EN, 23 Dec 1848; SHB II 294.
55. CB to EN, 12 April 1849; SHB II 324.
56. CB to WSW, 13 June 1849; SHB II 339.
57. CB to WSW, 25 June 1849; SHB II 348.

BOOK TWO: 1 (pages 109–17)

1. Peter Bayne, for example. See *Two Great English Women*; also May Sinclair, *The Three Brontës*.
2. M. Visick in *The Genesis of Wuthering Heights*, pp. 13–15.
3. F. E. Ratchford in *Gondal's Queen*, p. 37.
4. Visick, op. cit. pp. 17–20; Dorothy Van Ghent, *The English Novel*.
5. Van Ghent, op. cit.
6. The list is discussed by Isenberg, in *BST* XIV, pt 72.
7. F. E. Ratchford, *Gondal's Queen*, pp. 26, 41, etc.
8. *An Investigation of Gondal*, pp. 11–12.

BOOK TWO: 2 (pages 118–35)

1. CB's Preface to *Wuthering Heights*, 1850.
2. CB to WSW, 15 Feb 1848; SHB II 189.
3. Whone, in *BST* XI, pt 60.
4. Inscribed copy/copies, BPM Collection.
5. *The Sources of Wuthering Heights*.

6. Bradner, in *PMLA* March 1933.
7. Obituary, 'Currer Bell', in *Daily News*, April 1855; SHB IV 182.
8. *Blackwood's Magazine*, Nov 1840.
9. *Blackwood's Magazine*, Nov 1840.
10. Ibid.
11. CB to EN, 4 July 1834; SHB I 122.
12. Preface, *Wuthering Heights* (Collins, 1954).
13. Quoted Blondel, *Emily Brontë*.
14. *Revue des Deux Mondes*, 1857; also in *Ecrivains Modernes de l'Angleterre* (1887).
15. *BST* II, pt 15.
16. *Blackwood's Magazine*, June 1824 (Lockhart), and Feb 1839.
17. Op. cit. July 1824.
18. As suggested by Anne Lapraik Livermore, in *Quarterly Review*, 1962.
19. Moore, *Letters and Journals of Lord Byron* (1833) I.
20. Ibid.
21. Ibid.
22. Ibid.
23. CB to WSW, 16 April 1849; SHB II 327.
24. Wilson, in *Modern Quarterly Miscellany*, I (1947); Kettle, *The English Novel*.
25. 'Charlotte Brontë', in *ES* XIV (1929).
26. See, for instance, Gérin, *Charlotte Brontë* and Charlier, in *BST* XII, pt 65.

BOOK TWO: 3 (Pages 136–55)

1. *The Life and Works of Goethe*, book VI, ch. 7.
2. *Observer*, 16 March 1958.
3. 'Wuthering Heights', in *Early Victorian Novelists*.
4. Christian, 'The Brontës', in *Victorian Fiction, a guide to research*.
5. Day Lewis, in *BST* XIII, pt 67.
6. *NCF* Sept 1959.
7. *Pelican Guide*, VI.
8. *The English Novel*.
9. Klingopulos, in *Scrutiny*, XIV, no. 4 (1947).
10. Byron, 'The Dream'.
11. *Scrutiny*, XIV, no. 4 (1947).
12. Thrall, *Rebellious Fraser's*.
13. CB to PBB, 17 May 1831; SHB I 88.
14. *KR* IX, no. 4 (1947).
15. *NCF* XVII (June 1962).
16. *The Rise of the Novel*, ch. 7.
17. Solomon, in *NCF* XIV (June 1959).
18. Daiches, Introduction to *Wuthering Heights* (Penguin ed.).

19. Moser, in *NCF* XVII (June 1962).
20. Ibid.

BOOK THREE (pages 159–71)

1. *Critic*, 4 July 1846, p. 6.
2. *National Review*, V (July 1857).
3. CB to G. H. Lewes, 12 Jan 1848; SHB II 179–80.
4. *Life and Works of Goethe*, book VI, ch. II.
5. Stang, *The Theory of the Novel in England, 1830–1870*, p. 187.
6. *Fraser's Magazine*, LX (July 1859).
7. Lewes, loc. cit. note 4.
8. CB to Smith, 18 Sept 1850; SHB III 160.
9. *American Review*, June 1848 (G. W. Peck).
10. *NCF* XIV (March 1960).
11. *Athenaeum*, 28 Dec 1850.
12. *Economist*, 4 Jan 1851.
13. *Leader*, 28 Dec 1850.
14. CB to J. Taylor, 15 Jan 1851; SHB III 200.
15. D. G. Rossetti to W. Allingham, 19 Sept (1854?); *Letters*, ed. Birkbeck Hill (1897), pp. 58, 74, 125, 141. Dr J. Brown to Lady Trevelyan, 23 June 1851; *Letters*, ed. his son (1907) p. 87.
16. *Blackwood's Magazine*, July 1857, on 'Currer Bell'.
17. *National Review*, July 1857.
18. 'Thoughts on Modern English Literature', in *Fraser's Magazine*, LX (July 1859).
19. *Essays in Biography and Criticism*, 1st Series, 1857.
20. *La Revue des Deux Mondes*, X (1 and 15 July 1857); *Miss Brontë. Sa vie et ses œuvres*.
21. Gaskell to R. S. Oldham, 1 June 1857; Chapple and Pollard (ed.), *Letters of Mrs Gaskell*, no. 347A, p. 448.
22. F. M. Ford, *The English Novel*, p. 108.
23. H. Ludlam, *A Biography of Dracula* (1962).
24. *The Art of Fiction* (1884).
25. *Cornhill*, XXXVI (Dec 1877).
26. *Athenaeum*, June 1883.
27. See R. L'Hombreaud, *Arthur Symons* (1963) p. 278. Quotation from an unpublished manuscript by Arthur Symons.
28. *BST* II, pt 9 (1899).
29. *The Great Tradition*, p. 27 n.
30. *Nineteenth Century Minor Poets* (1967) Introduction.
31. Leavis, *The Great Tradition*, p. 27 n.
32. Douglas Duncan, *Emily Dickinson* (1965) p. 33.

Index

American Review on WH, 123, 162
Angria, 27
Arendt, Hannah, 83
Arnold, Matthew, 42; 'Haworth Churchyard', 166; 'A Wish', 166
Athenaeum on WH, 164
Atlas, 99, 165
Auden, W. H., 170
Austen, Jane, 120, 136, 161
Aykroyd, Tabitha ('Tabby'), 35

Balzac, H. de, 152
Bassompierre, Mlle, pupil in Brussels, 68
Baudelaire, C., 166
Bayne, Peter, journalist, 77, 80, 166
Beacon Hill, Halifax, 47
Bentley's Popular Novels, 134
Bewick, Thomas, 27
Birthday notes: Gondal allusions in, 109; of 1841, 60; of 1845, 57, 73, 76, 92, 112
Blackwood's Edinburgh Magazine, 28, 122, 126–8, 165
Blake, William, 9, 118
Bradford Observer, 105
Branwell family, and Methodism, 24
Branwell, Elizabeth, 32, 69, 71, 72, 120
Branwell, Maria (Mrs Brontë), 24
Brick, A. R., 163
Britannia, 99, 165
Brontë family: childhood, 19, 25, 27–28; and Haworth, 24; reading, 28, 33; and visual art, 26; and religion, 23–4; the records, location and dispersal, 10, 13, 17, 18, 19; their reputation, 13; and

romanticism, 170; state of Brontë studies, 9
Brontë, Anne: relationship to Emily, 29, 37, 55, 61; portraits of, 32, 33; birthday notes, 60, 61, 92; and Law Hill, 61; Agnes Grey, 92; Tenant of Wildfell Hall, 100
Brontë, Charlotte: and art, 134; and Brussels plan, 60, 61; early writing and novels, relationship, 115; account of EB, 10, 16; as critic of EB's works, 16–17, 99, 118, 118–20, 163–4; on artistic integrity, 25; as editor of her sisters' works, 16–17, 38, 51, 89, 90; on EB at Roe Head and Law Hill, 36–9, 54; letters to publishers, 91; and EB's poetry notebook, 87; reading list, 33, 123; and T. C. Newby, 97–8; Roe Head diary, 28; Biographical Notice of Ellis and Acton Bell, Editor's Preface to the New Edition of Wuthering Heights and Preface to the Literary Remains of Emily and Anne Brontë, 36–9, 87, 118, 121, 159, 160; 'Catalogue of My Books up to 1830', 27; 'Foundling', 29; Jane Eyre, 16, 68, 149, 163–4, 166; The Professor, 25, 92, 162; Shirley, 15, 34, 70, 163; Villette, 63, 72
BRONTË, EMILY JANE: childhood, 24–26; art and musical education, 26; early interest in Scott and Lockhart, 28; childhood culture in juvenilia by CB and PBB, 28;